How Would You Know My Whole Story...?

My story of overcoming severe childhood abuse

by

Shelby Rising Eagle

Contents

Acknowledgments	4
Editor's note	5
Forward	6
What you need to get your head around ...	6
Chapter 1. My family background	10
Mother	10
Father	10
My siblings	11
Into adulthood	12
Chapter 2. Marriage	16
Arizona and the birth of my children	19
My Father's illness	28
Back to California	32
Facing the darkness	33
Learning the truth	36
Goat Rock	40
Amy remembers our mother	40
Chapter 3. New beginnings	46
The Bishop	46
Jason's response	47
Divorce proceedings	48
Eric joins the family	49
A new home and first Christmas	50
Meeting church leaders	52
Child support and referral to Sarah	53
The children talk about their father	54
A turning point	55
Controlling mommy	58
The mother inside dies	59
Questioning my beliefs	60
The end with the Mormon Church	62
Chapter 4. All alone	64
New memories with Sarah	65
Martial arts lifestyle	69
Choosing friends and 'family'	71
Chapter 5. Empowerment	74
My family wants me back	74
Boundaries and job skills	76

Martial arts development	78
Spiritual matters	80
Leo	82
Aaron opens his school	83
Communication with my mother	84
Moving to Red Bluff	86
Leo makes life changes	87
Making friends	88
CHAPTER 6. QUESTIONING MY LIFE	**90**
Leo comes back	93
Drugs	94
CHAPTER 7.	
WORK AND THE EMPOWERED DYSFUNCTIONAL	**96**
Long-term care billing	99
Temping	100
Cardiology	100
Hospital billing	101
Jerrod's fall	101
2nd degree promotions	102
Tory's horses	105
My martial arts brother dies	106
CHAPTER 8. MY OWN SCHOOL	**108**
Starting My Own School	109
Aaron marries again	112
3rd degree promotions and falling out with Aaron	112
Training in San Francisco	115
CHAPTER 9. SPIRITUAL HEALING	**117**
Spiritual understanding	119
Bob	121
Brooke	123
CHAPTER 10. GIVING BACK WHAT WAS NEVER MINE	**126**
Closing the door	128
Retirement and my own horses	132
Making peace with old colleagues	134
Back to medical billing	135
My children as adults	136
CONCLUSIONS	**139**
Mary's thoughts:	140
REFERENCES	**141**

ACKNOWLEDGMENTS

I would first like to give thanks to my children, for the uncountable ways they have enriched my life. Thanks to my husband for his courage to make life changes and his steadfast support. I would also like to acknowledge my therapist, for walking with me through the darkest memories. Thanks to friends and colleagues for the lessons they have taught me. And thanks to my editor for the hours she spent making my words more accessible. To Mark and Denise I will always love you.

Shelby Rising Eagle

Editor's note

This is not a chronological story of Shelby Rising Eagle's entire life. Rather it is a series of events that were particularly relevant for the author during her growth from abuse victim, to proud survivor, to the unique person she is today. These events have been highlighted to present the reader with lessons from one woman's struggle to overcome a traumatic and abusive past. Because of the sensitivity of some subject matter, only analogies of actual sexual conduct have been included.

Out of respect for the privacy of others, all names used are fictional, some locations have been changed, and certain facts that were not directly relevant have been simplified or omitted. While the author has made every attempt to present a balanced view of the events in her life, this book is hers and as such represents her interpretations and feelings about that life.

Natasha Howard
California, 2007

Forward

Where do you begin telling a story so horrific, that the majority of people who would read it could never relate, let alone understand your words? Yet it is my story and it needs to be told to those who have lived a life like mine; those who struggle to find their way out of the darkness to find their light and claim their life as their very own. These people have a right and a need to know that they are not alone and that they can recover from these atrocities.

My words are very powerful for these beautiful people. Yet my words are poison to every remorseless perpetrator who hides the truth about what they do. I have chosen to present my words openly – in the light from which they hide. Perpetrators of these abuses are terrified that their victims could realize they have a right to their life. Such perpetrators do not want their victims to gain their own power and understand that they are not objects for anyone's religious beliefs or deviant behaviors. That awareness could destroy everything the perpetrators have done to control their victims' power for their own needs.

In my first book, How Would You Know, a story in poetry [1], I started with me, the little girl. I talked about how this little girl managed to survive parents who committed heinous atrocities not only on her but her siblings as well. In this book, I describe how this little girl became a woman, able to claim her own life. This is a true story, as accurate as I could make it. However, names and certain locations have been changed for protection.

What you need to get your head around ...

It may be difficult to accept, but my parents and other members of their cult are very deliberate and knowledgeable in methods of systematically traumatizing children to force them to disassociate. Once disassociation occurs, they can begin working with the splintered parts of the child's mind (created by the act of disassociation). In my case this knowledge of how to create and train disassociated alters was passed down through my mother's parents. I was born into a multi-generational Mormon cult of Satanic/ritual abuse. Some people have suggested that much of this knowledge came from experiments in systematic torture conducted by the Nazis. A brief internet search will provide as much information as you care to read on this topic.

I really do not care where it came from. What I care about is that it stops. Victims, whether or not from an organized cult, who have had to disassociate to survive the heinous actions of others, have the right to know that they can heal and claim their life. I hope that good people, who would never participate in anything like I experienced, can be educated to protect and empower themselves and share this awareness with others. That good people know what cult members do is the greatest deterrent for them. It will become harder for these evil people to confuse and distract others or present themselves as normal members of society. Shining the light on what they work hard to keep hidden is their worst nightmare. I want to give them this nightmare with the power of my voice.

The other factor to try to understand is disassociation. Many professionals continue to view anything other than their idea of "normal" behavior as a "disorder" [2]. I beg to differ with this narrow perspective of disassociation and will share my point of view for you to consider. You can decide for yourself.

First, you must recognize that there are people, like my parents and others in their cult, who are skilled in creating, training, and maintaining dissociated parts of a child's psyche, into adulthood. I am a product of this training, yet I still find this amazing. I did not even know that I was not in charge of my own life because of their careful training. Did any well-educated professionals work with any of these cult trainers before giving a 'disorder' label? Do professionals have the same views and in-depth knowledge of this type of training? I think not.

Let us consider what a disorder is, in my layman's terms. Is it when you have behaviors that undermine your ability to live a productive life? Is it a physical abnormality of the brain, preventing you

7

from responding within normal parameters so that you need medication to manage your life? Psychiatric professionals call people who use this ability to dissociate at varying levels Multiple Personality Disorder (MPD), or as it is now called Dissociative Identity Disorder (DID) [2]. That is nice, but is it a disorder? What about Dissociative Survival Skills?

There is obviously a difference between a disorder and a survival skill, but superficially, they may appear similar [3, 4]. People are generally recognized as developing DID from either sustained acts of extreme abuse by uncontrolled and abusive people or, as in my case, from systematic and ritualized trauma from earliest childhood. Our brains have the ability to dissociate to survive the horrors we experience. This Dissociative ability means we may not remember what happened, but in some way we are able to maintain our life in a productive manner.

Some people are able to dissociate, yet suffer additional neurological complications (bipolar disorder, schizophrenia) [4]. Something goes wrong in their brains. They constantly undermine themselves and are not able to live their lives without medical help. All of us who experienced sustained trauma as children still have the affects of being traumatized and still require therapy and recovery work. However, the difference is that some of us (for whatever reason) can live productive lives and others cannot manage life at all. No one really knows why, though some professionals have suggested that it may be related to intelligence (or more likely common sense). There is so much still to be learned in this area. Now ask yourself, "Is dissociation a disorder of the brain or a normal reaction of the brain in response to extreme trauma?" Where is the line between disorder and normalcy in dissociation?

Many professionals and laypeople have questioned why some people are able to survive, recover, and even thrive while others fail to do so [4]. In my world, our skilled perpetrators understood this concept. Those who did not survive their "training" were called breeders. They are controlled and used throughout their lives, and can be counted on to produce more "trainees." The ones that "survive"

8

mentally are used for more advanced purposes, usually significantly more abusive religious practices. This is what happened to me. My spiritual gifts and ability to survive made my father very powerful.

For me, over twenty years later, it seems that my life began when I was first married in 1980. Prior to marriage, I never realized how fractured my life really was. I only had bits and pieces of conscious memories, which did not fit together in any coherent time line. These were only a small part of what I later remembered of a lifetime, swallowed in a black hole of memories so horrific some will never be recovered.

I still marvel at the fact that I am alive and able to live my life at all. Why am I alive after all the terrible things that were done to me? The only answer that makes sense is that I was a fighter. I never gave in and I never gave up. This was the one thing that my parents feared in me and could never control.

My soul is like one of those warrior women in fantasy pictures; with long flowing hair and great strength, holding a sword in hand and ready to fight for what is right and valiant with no fear of the battle ahead. Of course, I always felt she must have a noble steed ready to carry her anywhere. I cannot express to you how strong my soul is, and I have since realized that few people can relate to such strength. Nevertheless, it is my soul and now my hardest challenge is often to find a balance between the warrior and the graceful woman who grew from her.

This is my story ...

Shelby Rising Eagle
California, 2007

CHAPTER 1. MY FAMILY BACKGROUND

Mother

Betsy Leonard was born in 1924, into a deeply Mormon family in Utah. She is related to one of the Mormon prophets on her mother's side, the side of the family from which the abuse originated. Because this is multi-generational ritual abuse, my mother is a very disturbed person. However, she always seemed to know how to present herself publicly as a decent and functional person. I have recovered memories of my maternal grandmother and maternal uncle also being involved and sexually assaulting me in my grandmother's house with my mother and father actively participating. While the Satanic ritual abuse originated on my mother's side, my father and other church members willingly chose to be involved.

Father

Jason Thompson was born in 1923 and raised in a small town in northern California. The youngest of four siblings, he had no specific religious upbringing. He was quick-witted, loving to 'hug redheads, tease the ladies, and tell jokes,' and had a strong sense of family pride and heritage. With such a solid background, where did he go so wrong? I will never know. I can only clarify some dynamics that may make sense.

I don't know anything about my paternal grandfather; who died before I was born, but my grandmother Irene was born in the late 1800's and was not allowed to attend college. As was common in that era, at 14 years old she was married to a man 20 years her senior. She was a very intelligent woman caught in an era that did not allow women to achieve their dreams or intellectual potential. She became very bitter and dominated my father (some professionals have suggested that the dynamics of sexual abuse between them). She did not like my mother and attempted to get my father to come back to their small town to live close to her. Unfortunately, every attempt

10

on her part backfired. She hated my mother, so I suspect she saw right through her and wanted to save her son. However, my grandmother's attempts to get him away from Betsy only seemed to push him closer and he never saw any wrong in her.

Unlike his domineering mother, the Mormon Church offered a patriarchal society. It was an easy hook for his needy ego - he could be the man of divine authority. Between the pressures of these two dynamics was his downfall. I really believe he knew what he got himself into and would not or could not get out of it. I remember him saying sometimes that he was going to Hell after he died and it would be his own fault. I never understood as a child or teenager what he meant, but later during recovery those words were very validating to me.

My siblings

Lawrence is eighteen years older than I am. When I was born, he was preparing to go on a mission for the Mormon Church. When he returned, he took off his temple garments and left the Church. He was the child who went astray in my parent's eyes. I have few memories of him due to the age difference between us, but I considered him a great brother and all that I do remember about him was good.

Amy, my only sister, is fourteen years older than I am. My mother made her take care of me, which she resented. She felt that if she was going to take care of a child, it should be her own. When she was fifteen, she got pregnant and it was a way for her to get out of the house. I remember calling Amy „Mom" and never acknowledged my own mother as „Mom".

Jason Jr. is twelve years older than I am and was always the holy brother. He was named after our dad and became an extension of my father's ego and pride. He represented what my father always wanted to be or thought he was. He was a quiet one and would rather walk out the back door than fight or cause conflict.

Jake is five years older than I am and was always the lost brother. He was lost in the family structure, never causing conflict but never walking out the backdoor either. He just blended in and wandered aimlessly in life.

I am Shelby, the youngest of the five children. By the time I came, the others were well on their ways to getting away from home. I was the only child who always stood up to my parents. I was the fighter, even when I was a toddler. I stood up to them, only to find more that I was punished more in order to make me conform. Mostly it was Jake and I. We were far enough apart in age that due to the extreme abuse we never bonded with each other. We just survived our parents by any means necessary.

To me, my life began when I was 18 and able to get out on my own. I just remember feeling that I had to get away in order to make my life better. I didn't understand why I felt that way. To me, my prior life was a blur of bad experiences that I wanted to free myself from and start over. This is the reason I start my story of recovery at this stage of my life.

Into adulthood

I was nineteen and finally able to get out of the house and rent an apartment with a roommate. I did not have any life skills and my education was very limited despite having a High-school diploma. I was barely able to read, because of learning disabilities that were only diagnosed much later in my life. Of course, my parents did not want me to be successful because that would reduce my dependence on them. Besides, I was a girl and thus not as important as my father's sons. He considered his sons most important and made sure they got every opportunity for education. I always fought about this with my dad - how his sons were more important than I was. When I was a teen, I fought with him all the time and hated him. I do not regret any of my rebellious behavior. He deserved every bit of it and more.

My mother was the catalyst for many of these fights and always played the victim. I did not recognize the dynamics in my home nor did I have any conscious memory of the abuse happening to me that never stopped. I knew there was something wrong but I could never put my finger on what it was. I always thought that I was the problem and not my parents. I felt that it must be me and I was crazy to think that there was something wrong – Why, I came from a family that belonged to the only true church of God so therefore the problem had to be me. Mom always kept me confused and lied about what was happening. I hated the situation and just wanted to get away from my family, start my own life, and have something better. I always felt as if I had one foot in a spiritual realm. It was much later that I discovered why I felt this way and how I had been so horrifically abused.

There were only two things that were really important to me at that time. In high school, Vanessa was my best friend in the whole world. We did drill team together and talked about our deepest feelings (what we wanted in life, how we didn't want to be like our parents). I did not have many friends, but Vanessa always stood by me. Even though she was not Mormon, she was my best friend. After high school she went to Brigham Young University (BYU) Hawaii then BYU Utah. In college she converted to Mormonism and was then married in the temple. Our friendship was very important to me.

After I left the church we did stay friends but could not keep it going. I am not sure why. Probably because she believed in the church and I no longer did. She has stayed in the church and her husband never liked me. Even though she will have nothing to do with me now, she will always be a special person in my life, whom I will always love.

The other important part of my life was my horses. I owned horses since I was fourteen. I was so rebellious at that time that my parents got me a horse to keep some control over me and stop me from running away. Through my teenage years, my horses were the one thing that kept me going and that I connected to. Barrel racing was my one success that made me feel that I was something. My parents supported the bare minimum with my horses. To learn how to ride, I cleaned stalls in exchange for lessons. I rode to the local horse club arena to barrel race. The arena was twelve miles away. I rode there to barrel race and come home alone, with no support from my parents. One of the horse club members befriended me and started taking me to shows. I made friends with his daughters and it was one of the few times in my youth that I have happy memories. Once I became friends with other horse people, my parents took more interest in my activities. Probably to look as if they supported their daughter. I was always out of the house and away from my parents, riding my horse and dreaming of being somewhere or someone else.

I have always been a very spiritual person and have seen angels on several occasions. The first time I was 16 years old and we had moved to Colorado. My horse was to be shipped over and according to my father, Momma Star had a stroke before she was shipped and died. I was devastated at losing my best friend. As I drove home I looked in the rearview mirror and saw an angel with my horse. I cried and cried and told her that I would miss her and wished she could be with me. I do not remember driving, but was safe all the same.

The second time I was still in Colorado and at my aunt's house to share Family Home Evening. My uncle gave a lesson and when I looked up I saw an angel standing in the room. He was dressed in white to the floor but did not stand on the ground. I was shocked and then tried to say hello, but he disappeared. My uncle told me he could feel the spirit in the room and wanted to know if I saw it.

The third time, I was attending Rick's College in Idaho and could feel an evil spirit in my dorm room. The air kept getting heavier and heavier as I walked in my room and it was hard to breathe. When I went to bed, I saw books sliding off the shelf. I called my dad, who said that if they want to move books off the shelf I should put the books on the floor! Obvious but weird advice. I put all the books on the floor, but it got harder and harder to breathe when I was in my room. It took all my strength to get out of my room. It kept getting worse, so I asked my home teachers to come and bless my room and to give me a blessing as well. After the blessing the heaviness was gone from my room and before I fell asleep I could see three angels. Two were standing at the side of my bed and the other one was standing at the end of my bed facing away. I felt like they were there to protect me, though I never knew why this happened.

Chapter 2. Marriage

I was a devout Mormon and believed in the teachings with all my heart. I knew without any doubt that this was the only true church of God on earth. How could I have known anything different when that was what I was taught to believe? I was only kept in Mormon circles and knew nothing about a non-Mormon world. Everything in my world and family was connected with Mormonism. Though I'd had a couple of boyfriends, I just wanted to get married so that I could make the right Mormon choices and have a better life. I did not want to be like my sister's kids who were near to my age. They were either on drugs, getting pregnant or drunk while still in their teens. I wanted to be like my brother Jason. He was successful, with a college degree at BYU in child psychology and family relations, and work with Latter Day Saints (LDS) Social Services. I really respected him as my example of success. His wife Sally always preached to me that I must get married in the temple and have children to be a good Mormon and follow Christ's teachings. It was hard being on my own because I kept messing up my checkbook, running short of money, or having my car break down. I did not manage my life very well at all. In my heart I knew I wanted to find someone or something better than what I had. I wanted to step up in life and I believed that I could do just that.

I met Scott Jennings in the Young Adults program at church. He was not a "fox" but he was not bad looking either. He seemed to be a very nice person with a family that appeared well off. They had a very nice home and his father had a high paying job. They drove expensive cars and exemplified the successful upper-middle class Mormon family. Certainly this was a step up in life. Scott's dad was Eugene Jennings, a large stoic man of whom I had a fearful awe. Everyone in his family obeyed what he said without question. It was subservience. Scott's mother, Evelyn, was a short woman and exemplified the good Mormon wife. Scott's older brother, Wayne, was the family failure. He could not keep a job for long and never had a successful marriage. Scott's younger sister, Kathy, was a plump bright teenager.

16

I don't remember Scott asking me to marry him, but I do remember asking when we are going to tell his parents. I wanted to escape my single life so much that I took the first offer, which on the outside seemed to be a great situation. Scott was a returned missionary and got a degree in electrical engineering and a job with a top telecommunications company before we were married. He was my knight in shining Mormon armor. I knew without a doubt that I had made all the right decisions by all the right Mormon standards, so my life was going to be successful with bliss and happiness forever. I had no idea of the darkness that I lived in, or what I would have to go through to get out.

Scott and I were married in the Oakland Temple in September of 1980. His job was in San Jose so we moved from Chico. Prior to our marriage he could not keep his hands off me. He was always pushing the limits of our Mormon propriety and rushing to sex. After marriage our sex life slowly stopped. We would have sex two to three times a month at most. It bothered me, but I did not have anything to compare it with or any real idea that there might be something wrong. I dove into his family and worked hard at fitting in.

I never did fit in though, and was only politely tolerated. Soon after our marriage, Scott started to tell me that I had not been raised with good manners and that my family was trailer park trash. He explained that my behavior was coarse, which was why I would never fit into upper class circles. To Scott I was more of an embarrassment than an asset. I took what he said to heart, not wanting to be a wife that was an embarrassment to him, and set out to learn better social behavior. Evelyn tried to help, but I was never able to be like her. She was the queen of snobbery and always disconnected from any emotions. She read books and talked about other church member's lives and how they had troubles and not her.

I wanted to be a good wife and follow the teachings of God's only true Church. Now that I was married, my sister-in-law Sally began pressuring me to have a child and it was not long before I was pregnant. Scott took the news of my pregnancy as life's failure. I had never realized his obsession to be just like his dad. He needed to have the same job his whole life, the same house to raise his kids in, the same everything. He had a blinding need to be just like his father. To Scott, a child meant that he could not buy a home, wouldn't have job stability, would never find any success, and would be seen as a failure in his dad's eyes. Anything that stood in the way of walking in his dad's footsteps made him a complete failure. It was extreme thinking and I could not understand at all. I had experienced many "failures" in life but I picked myself up and moved on without considering myself a failure. Scott would not consider any reasoning that differed from "his father's footsteps."

I will never forget going to his parent's house for our first Christmas. I was excited to share the great news that I was pregnant. However, Scott was not willing to tell his parents and I felt very hurt. Instead, I went to my parents' house and told them. They seemed very happy for me and I felt a little less alone in my pregnancy. I had horrible morning sickness everyday. Like clockwork I would make friends with the ceramic bowl all morning. When we went to stay with his parents I had a flu as well as morning sickness. Evelyn saw the state I was in and asked Scott about me. He took her to the garage to inform her I was pregnant. I felt really insulted and hurt that this was how he informed his mother. What happened to life's wonderful moments and sharing the joy of having your first child... especially since we were married!

After Scott told her I was pregnant she was really angry. She stormed into my room yelling that I was ruining her son's life by having a child so soon. I was lying in bed sick and completely shocked. What had happened to the Mormon values of having children and that a child is not something that ruins your life? Then she told me that she never stayed in bed with morning sickness so I'd better get out of bed and stop acting like a baby. I refused to get out of bed because I felt sick and it was all I could do to run to the bathroom and back to my room. Here I believed I was in such a wonderful family, a big step up in life and I get a mother-in-law yelling that I am pregnant and ruining her son's life. I was really hurt by her behavior. Eugene never said a word about my pregnancy. Then again he never said anything to me in the first place. I just wanted to go back home and made Scott take me home early to spend our first Christmas with each other instead of his family. It was a horrible Christmas.

Arizona and the birth of my children

Not long after Christmas, Scott told me that his company was moving his department to Tempe, Arizona. We took a trip to Arizona to look for places to live. I really liked Arizona and saw at it as a way to get away from both his family and mine. It was a new adventure for me, a chance for a better life with my husband. I believed things would get better once we moved, so we packed up everything including my horse and moved to Arizona. I found a place to board my horse and continued to ride until I gave birth.

After we moved into our new home in Gilbert I set to work making up a room for my baby. Scott was not interested in helping me to get ready for the baby. He did not want to talk about names and said it would be a waste of time until the baby came. I felt really hurt that Scott was so uninvolved emotionally in the birth of his first child. I really felt that I was all alone in having my baby and had no one to share what was to me a wonderful event in my life. He did not care what I did to get ready for the baby as long as he was not bothered about it.

In 1981 I gave birth to a beautiful boy and named him Mark Jennings. He had lots of black hair and weighed 6lbs 7oz. He seemed so tiny, and I remember taking him in my arms and telling him that I would love him always. I also remember him crying in the hospital and I panicked because I did not know what to do with such a tiny baby. I realized then that he was completely dependent on me and that my life would change forever. I loved taking care of him. He was my whole world. My mother came to help me with Mark and the recovery from childbirth. I tried to do everything as soon as I'd given birth and realized that my body was not strong enough to go back to what I was accustomed to. It was about five weeks before I felt really recovered.

19

After my mother left Scott's parents came and Mark was blessed in the Mormon Church by his Dad with his Grandfather at his side. When Scott's parents came I was expecting the judgments about what a bad person I was for ruining their son's life. Instead, nothing was said and they went back to tolerating me and welcomed the baby. I thought it odd that they were so angry at me for being pregnant but no longer upset when the baby came. The other thing I considered very odd was that they always said Mark looked like me and nothing like Scott. Yet when I would look at Scott's baby pictures there was no doubt about the resemblance to his son. Through the years as my children grew. Scott's mother never acknowledged any Jennings family resemblance in my children. Nonetheless, Mark is the spitting image of his dad whether they accept it or not.

As time went on Scott's depressive episodes never let up. The current reason for his depression was that I was spending too much money and that it was my fault he didn't earn enough. He acted as if, by being late in paying a bill, there would be a man with a big black marker just waiting to put the infamous black mark on his credit report that would spread like wild fire making him a failure. These bouts of depression went on for years. He was inconsolable and it began to take a toll on me and Mark. Scott had a habit of drawing pictures of people hanging dead or body parts cut off from the main torso. I found these drawings odd and disturbing, but when I questioned him he replied that there was nothing unusual since he'd been doing this since he was little boy. Scott never bonded with Mark or felt the need to spend time with him. In fact he had little patience with Mark. Scott continued to tell me that no matter what the problem was it was my fault that he was a failure. It was like a ritual. Every day he would come home and inform me that I was stupid and an embarrassment and the reason he was not successful. No matter how hard I tried to help Scott feel better he never did. It was a vicious cycle that was hard to live with or get out of, and only resulted in me being the reason why he was on the verge of being an absolute failure.

As Mark got older I began to notice that he was not keeping up with his speech development. He was two years old and not talking. I went to his pediatrician and he just kept telling me there was nothing wrong and Mark was being stubborn or would grow out of it. I was told over and over by people that he would grow out of it, but he didn't grow out of it. His doctor was wrong. It only got worse. When he did try to talk he would only repeat what I said. By the time he was 2 ½ he started having screaming fits. He never called me Momma, and never talked to me. He continued to live in his own world and just repeat what I said.

I decided to go to a different doctor and have him evaluated. This is when I started to get some help for him. He started to go to a private special-education preschool. The lady who ran the school had been taught in Germany to work with children like Mark. She was able to teach him to use the toilet and got him to stop his screaming fits at school. As I look back, I find it amazing that not one professional ever talked to me about Autism. He had every symptom but instead he was given every disability label except the one he really had - Autism. It appeared to me that if the doctors could not see an obvious physical disability then it must not exist. I also remember church members looking at me in disgust, like 'What is that boy's problem?' or 'Why doesn't she just spank him and make him behave?' I would get a lot of looks from other mothers in church and they were always ready to let me know that he was just stubborn and I needed to have firmer hand on him to make him stop acting like that. I began to feel that if one more person told me to spank him I was going to explode and beat the crap out of them to see how well they actually liked violence and what message they got from my fists being knocked upside their heads! I started to notice that when Scott watched Mark while I rode my horse, I would come home to find bruises on Mark's body. When I asked Scott what happened he always had an excuse.

I became pregnant again. I had to sell my horse because Mark was taking so much of my time that I could not make time for both him and my horse with another child on the way. Selling my horse was one of the hardest things I ever did. He was my best friend and confidant, always listening and taking my worries away. He always made me feel better. I might have the worries of the world on my shoulders, but if I rode my horse all the stress and worries just melted away. My horse was the emotional anchor in my life. I sold him to a ranch in Colorado through another church member. I heard from time to time how well he was doing on the ranch, but I never felt the same after I sold him. For many years I would break down crying because I missed my horse and this special connection with my best friend. It felt like a piece of my soul had been cut out and tossed away.

Something very special happened during both of my pregnancies. While I was pregnant I could feel my children's spirit, I felt their personalities, when they were happy or sad, and I knew whether they were a boy or a girl. When they were born their spirits left me and stayed in the baby that I'd given birth to. I will never forget how their spirits stayed with me during pregnancy. It was a very special experience. In November of 1983 I gave birth to a beautiful baby girl. Victoria had long black hair and weighed 8lbs 12oz. I called her Tory. I now had a baby to take care of and a child I needed to run after all day long.

My fourth experience with angels happened sometime after Tory was born and I was going through one of my hard times with Scott. I was depressed and wanted to leave and start a new life. I dreamt that I heard an Angel talking and could feel I was in a better place free from hate and anger. There are no words to describe the peace I felt. The angel asked if I wanted to come home. I thought about it and then about my children. I told him I did not want to go home now because I loved my children and would not abandon them. So I woke up back in Arizona with my kids.

Mark was like four children in one. He was a very busy child and I always had to be vigilant. When I needed a break I would let him play with the sprinkler knobs in the backyard. He was completely fascinated with how he could turn a knob and water would come up out of the ground. With little professional help and not really knowing what was going on with my child I decided to think through what I could do to help this child I loved so much. I wanted to connect with Mark and decided that since I could not bring him to my world I needed to go into his. I would spend hours with him in the sandbox or make roads and play with cars. He would look at me in wonder and then slowly start to play with me. It was more of a parallel playing but he played all the same. I felt that I was making some kind of breakthrough by joining him in his world. This was the first time that I had made a big impression on him and it seemed that we connected. I considered it a great success and a start in helping my son. After being together awhile, Mark began to take green bar computer paper and spread it through the house. He drew streets and houses, naming all the roads and numbering the houses. He played with his cars on the paper and was in his own world. He never connected with me in this medium but took what we'd done in the sand box and turned it into something new. When he was finished he would fold the computer paper very carefully. The next day he would unfold and put it back in the same way he'd had it the day before. Mark was amazing with numbers, putting things together, or music beats. When he was only three, he could put 60-piece puzzles together and then take them apart turn the pieces over and put the puzzle back together on the reverse side. He would take the knobs off all my dressers and any other pieces of furniture that knobs, lay them out carefully and then go back through the house and put them back on. He played with blocks and would cry in frustration and start screaming if he could not get them to line up the way he thought they should. One day he got up early, pulled out a frying pan, cracked the eggs into the pan, and threw away the egg shells. He put bread in the toaster and got butter and jelly out. When I got up a few minutes later he was standing on a chair with a spatula in hand waiting for the eggs to cook. Thank God he did not know how to turn on the stove.

It was important for Mark to finish what he started. If he could not finish he would explode with screams for up to two hours. His little brain would short circuit and he could not stop. I felt really helpless and frustrated that I could not make things better for him. When we went to the warehouse stores with every isle numbered, Mark counted the numbers as I went through the aisles. One day I was short on time and could not go down every aisle for him. I tried to explain that we could not count the numbers today because I was in a hurry, but Mark could not handle it and started screaming. It was so hard standing in line while he screamed. I got so many looks from "what is your son's problem?" to "you bitch" to "you poor thing". It always amazes me that most people did not understand special-needs children and would make horrible judgments. That day Mark continued to cry all they way home and for another hour after. I learned the hard way that it was easier to go down every aisle and just let him finish what he started. One day, Mark got into the honey, not just a jar but a gallon jar. He spilled it all over the kitchen floor and I had to scoop it up with a dust pan before I could mop it up. Another time Mark found the powdered sugar. He stood on a chair in the middle of the kitchen and shook the box until the whole kitchen was covered from ceiling to floor.

Mark never did anything in a small way. He loved yarn and would take about six skeins and tie them from one tree to another, then a plant, then a pole, then to something else. By the time he ran out he had yarn strung everywhere and the whole house tied in yarn from back to front. I did not understand his reasons but I took it in stride and enjoyed his creativity. I had to laugh at a lot of things he did. You either went crazy or you found humor in these situations and what your child did. Once without thinking it through I got him a waterbed. He saw where the hose went into the bed and during the first night in his new bed Mark took the sheets off and unscrewed the plug. He was up all night slowly letting the water seep out of his bed. When I got up the next morning and stepped into the hallway my feet were wet. I was shocked to see water all the way down the hallway, into the front room and the dining room. I saw that it went through the walls from Mark's room. When I went inside he was sitting beside the plug looking very happy with what he was doing. I just picked him up, bathed and dressed him. I could not get angry at him. He was doing what any curious child would do, playing with water. I called the carpet people to clean up the mess and by the end of the day the bed was sold and a new bed purchased that did not contain water. Lessons learned when you have a very intelligent and active child. I had to laugh or go crazy. That was how I dealt with the stress.

I never gave up on Mark because I loved him. Mark had screaming sessions 4 to 6 times a day from age 2½ to six years of age. The first parenting class I went to I listened to mothers complaining that their kids said "no" or would not listen. When I began to talk about my son and his screaming fits the room became quiet and the other mothers' faces were full of shock. I felt very out of place and knew these women had no idea about a child with behavior problems. I questioned whether I was in the right class. This was another time in which I realized that I had a child who needed more help than a parenting class could offer. As a result I was even more determined to help my son and do what ever it took to help him. I was going to make sure that he overcame whatever his handicap was. I was determined that I could help him overcome this and be a normal child. Scott harassed me to put him in a psychiatric facility and never stopped trying to convince me to give him up. Scott viewed Mark as a personal defect, a reminder to Scott that he could not produce a normal male child and thus a reflection of his manhood. My feeling was that Mark was my son and I could not give him up to God knows who. And how could I know he would be safe? No one was going to hurt my child and no one loved him as much as I did. He was my child and I was NEVER going to give up on him.

When Mark was old enough to start Kindergarten I remember taking him to be evaluated. Mark ran into the room, stuck out his arm and knocked everything off of every table in the room. When I came running in behind him with the baby in my arms he was circling for round two. As I ran in in after Mark, this wonderful lady came up, took me by my shoulders and sat me down. She looked at me and said she would take Mark in her class and she understood what I was going through. I just started to cry. The tears began to flow like a dam had broken. I had no friends who understood a child like Mark and as a result I had no one to talk to. Finally I'd met a per-

25

son who knew what I was going through. Her name was Judy and she told me she had raised two boys like Mark. She was so much help to me in understanding Mark and how to work with him. Mark did not get easier, but I learned how to work with him and not against him.

As I reflect back, I realize my son was the one who saved my life. I was referred to Social Services, who sent a counselor named Mary to my home to help me with Mark. This was the beginning of my getting out of the darkness I lived in. Here I was doing everything to save him, not realizing that Mark was saving me. It was a slow process for me to see the abusive relationship I was in. I had no boundaries and did not see how I allowed Scott to walk all over me emotionally. It was hard to see any of this. I poured all of my strength into my son while dealing with a husband who fought me every step of the way.

As a result of Mary's help, Scott became more violent. His behavior was getting out of control and Mark started having bruises again. These were not one or two little bruises from time to time either. I realized Scott was getting worse one day after I came home from work at the barn and got Mark ready for bed and saw that he had bad bruises on his bottom where Mark had spanked him. He also had finger marks on his face. I was so angry at Scott for hurting my child and I was tired of listening to his pathetic excuses. I blew up and we fought. The next day I showed Mary, the counselor, the bruises. She said I would have to turn Scott in or I would lose my help with Mark. My child came first and I turned Scott in. Child Protective Services (CPS) decided to do nothing about it because of what I was doing for Mark. I wished CPS would have taken steps to make Scott go to anger management classes but apathy always seems to rule county services.

I told Scott that I'd reported him and he was being investigated. He really blew up and asked how I could do that to him when he was such a good dad. He explained that I had betrayed him by making him look like the bad guy when it was me who was the problem. Once again, even when all proof proved otherwise, it was still my fault. I kept getting counseling from Mary despite Scott's telling me Mary did not know what she was talking about and that it was

Mary who was ruining our marriage. Scott really fought and continually told me that I was the problem in this marriage because of the stupid family I came from. He hated my family and insisted they were the reason I was an embarrassment to him and his family.

To protect my children I began to change. If I saw the slightest bruise on one of them I began to threaten Scott that I would beat the crap out of him. I made it very clear to him that I would not allow my children to be abused. When I started to threaten him with physical violence he began to be much more careful about what he did to my children. A couple of times when we fought I pushed him around and I began to see a side of me that was very strong. I was surprised that I had this in me. Scott was also surprised to see me get physically aggressive with him. He was not a fighter and was not sure what to do. Scott was a coward who did not understand how to deal with violence, not like I did. I told him that he would never hit my children again and demanded that he start counseling to get help with his anger issues. If he did not I would turn him in again and make sure that he was prosecuted. This was the beginning of my becoming aware of the warrior woman inside me whom I'd never consciously known. This warrior began to appear and Scott was afraid of her. He became more careful and made sure that he didn't leave any bruises that I could see. He changed from abusive to passive aggressive actions. Although I did not realize it then, he became even more abusive towards Mark and Tory. These tactics were the beginning of Mark shutting down completely. When Scott started his usual "You're the reason for all my problems" I began to use what I learned from counseling. I began to say that I was not responsible for his anger issues and failures in life. These were my first steps towards disengaging from his cycle of abuse.

As Mark and Tory got older I had been able to work at a stable and ride horses again. I learned dressage and was able to teach, train and ride up to fourth level dressage. This was a special time for me and I still value the great opportunity I had to learn from a great rider and trainer. To help protect my children I got up early in the morning while they and Scott were sleeping to ride the horses that needed to be trained. I rode five to six horses and was home by 7:00 am. Due to the Arizona heat everyone rode either at midnight or started at 4:00 am. If I needed to go to the barn in the evenings I took my children with me.

My Father's illness

At about that same time my father became very sick. He had suffered three heart attacks in the past and was on disability. He hated not working and considered himself less of a man because he could not work and take care of his family. My parents had returned to California from Louisiana a few years before, because my father could no longer work due to his heart condition. He was very depressed and since he lived with my sister we all had to hear about it. He refused to get out of bed and was talking about killing himself. I don't know what got in me but I got really angry at him and knew he was full of shit. I took a knife into his room and tossed it on his bed, saying if he wanted to die he should just go ahead and get it done, "Everyone here is tired of your feeling sorry for yourself and whining." I told him to slash his wrist vertically so no one could fix his veins to ensure he died. I walked out of the room and left my sister's house. He got out of bed after that and stopped his self-indulgent whining for a little while.

My dad had addictive behaviors and food was first on his list. He did not take care of himself properly. He would be the first person at the table to eat and the last to leave. He loved food and always ate large amounts. I have two significant memories about my father and his addiction to food. My dad loved Snickers and would buy a bunch of them and hide them inside and outside the house. I found his secret stash and would put them on the coffee table and eat them in front of him, acting as if I had no idea whose they were or why they were there. He would storm out of the room absolutely livid. Later he would hide more Snickers. Once when I was a senior in high school, I was in bed and got this feeling to crack open the door and look in the kitchen. I watched my dad sneak into the kitchen, looking around furtively to see if anyone was watching. No one was in the room, the curtains were closed, and my mother was already asleep. He went to the cupboard, got out a large bowl, then slowly poured cereal into the bowl. He was facing the corner of the kitchen with his back to the room. As he slowly poured cereal and milk he would look behind him to see if anyone was watching. Then he stood facing the corner of the kitchen eating his cereal and checking that no one heard or saw him. Being 18 years old I found this hysterical, and ran and laughed into my pillow so no one would hear me. Suddenly I stopped, realizing that I did the same thing.

I was always conscious of my weight and had addictive behaviors with food that I did not fully understand at the time. My mother always told me that I was fat and ugly and never looked good in anything, so I had a huge complex about not looking good. For the first time I realized I had the same problem as my dad with food. Evern though I wasn't overweight, I considered myself fat and swore to myself there would be no sneaking food and getting away with it. If I overate then it would show by my being overweight, so I reconciled myself to no longer hide the food I ate. Of course, it took me years to get food to stop controlling me. It was a very hard process and to this day I still love to eat. Denial? Not really, I no longer have the need to eat or I feel like I will die. I no longer feel desperate to eat. Addictions are very hard to overcome and it never really goes away.

I hated my father for as long as I could remember. I wanted him to acknowledge me for me, not, "I love you like my sons." He always believed boys were more important than girls were. Through the years, we fought all the time and he went out of his way to make me mad to the point I wanted to kill him. He used to upset me by sucking on his teeth or smacking his food with his mouth open. He knew that what he was doing would make me furious and did it with the pretence of "oh I forgot." I would get so angry I would call him names and leave the room. I realized later through memory work when this started. When I was a toddler, he would force me up to his face and either chew gum or eat food with his mouth open smacking away or sucking on his teeth right next to my right ear. He kept

29

doing this until I was hysterical, screaming for him to stop. He did that to punish me when I was little. I later realized he never stopped using this to punish me. Even as I type these words, I feel the pain in my right ear and anger rages inside of me. I do not think I will every get over that body memory. He was a very vindictive man and he did this to make himself feel powerful over me.

In 1985, my mom and dad came to Arizona to visit me. I was not thrilled to have my dad in my house, but was able to tolerate him. It was almost as if he knew he was dying soon and tried to make peace. I would have none of what I felt were phony attempts to appease his guilty conscience. Little did I realize until much later that he and mom never stopped abusing me and memories of this visit were validated during my recovery. In 1986, he died from chronic heart failure secondary to diabetes and I flew to California for the funeral. I remember feeling no need to cry at the service. His death was a relief to me, though I tried to act sad and to comfort my mom. I've always found it amazing how when someone dies they suddenly become saints. My mom had always complained about him but once he was dead she couldn't live without him. When we buried him in the town where he was raised, there was a moment in the eulogy where someone could mention some positive experience of my dad. All of us siblings stood there and said nothing. It became uncomfortable until Jake finally told some story about our dad. The graveside service ended quickly after this.

While I was in Chico for the funeral, Evelyn, my mother-in-law, started talking about her older son, Wayne. He was having problems with his marriage and she began to talk about how he used to hide pornography and women's underwear in his room since he was thirteen. I remember feeling shocked, like here's another sign of what is wrong with this family, but I still couldn't put my finger on it.

Between Scott and his depressions, his anger towards my children and finding out about his brother, it became more and more clear to me that his family was not what they appeared to be. I started to believe in myself and decided it wasn't me who had the "problem." Looking back, I'm still amazed at how blind I was to the dysfunction

I lived in and the extremely abusive people in my life. If dysfunction is your normalcy then how do you recognize that your "functional" really is "dysfunctional." It always amazes me how functional dysfunction can appear if that is what you are used to. When you are raised with violence and dysfunctional abusive behaviors, this is your normalcy. If you have never experienced anything else how do you know what is wrong or abusive? This was me.

I began to realize how much of my life I didn't remember. The black hole holding my suppressed memories was always there, I just didn't know how to see it. How can you see what is subconsciously there? You don't remember so you don't see it. This is the best way I can explain it. As Mary continued to work with me, I slowly became conscious of this black hole in my life that my parents had worked hard for me not to see. The more I learned about parenting skills, working with my son's disabilities, the more I opened the doors to a world I never knew. I slowly began to see a difference in how I was raised and what I was being taught by Mary. The more doors I opened the more Scott fought me. He worked hard to invalidate what I was learning. His reasoning remained that I was the stupid one with the ignorant family while he came from the perfect family with no problems. It was as if he was afraid of what I would come to understand. Little did I know how true this really was.

I used to pour out in my journal how much I hated my dad and about my marriage. When I read my journal now, I see the changes in my marriage as I got counseling. Prior to counseling, I would write about what a great marriage I had and how much better my life was. With counseling I realized I wrote about the changes in our marriage that became obvious as I got help for Mark. This journal was very validating to me later and to the police when Scott was investigated again for child abuse. The journal validated me and was the reason the Chico Sheriff's department supporting me in keeping my kids.

Back to California

In 1987, Scott's work moved his department back to Chico. Since I felt so alone in caring for my kids I wanted to move back nearer my family. I was desperate for any kind of support. I was homesick and constantly called my mom to talk about my marriage and my son. I thought it would be better to go back home and start over, that maybe it would be better with extended family. We returned, planning to use the money from the house we sold in Arizona for a down payment on a new home in California. We soon found a small but very nice house in a good neighborhood. I checked every school district's special education programs so I could make informed decisions about the right place for my son. I really liked this house and the school district had a good special education program.

We didn't have quite enough money for the down payment and I remember Scott telling his parents about the options to buy this home. His parents just sat and listened, making no offer to help their son and Scott would never stand up to his dad or ask for help. I got so angry watching this scene play out yet again – the parents coldly and silently watching their son who needed help. I started shouting at Eugene for being so cold. I told him that if he loved his son like anyone else on this earth loves their children, he would be glad to offer money to help his son buy a house. With all the money he had why couldn't he break open his wallet to help his own son? Of course, this went over like a lead balloon. I got a cold glare for my insolence, but I didn't back down. I was sick and tired of this family doing nothing. Finally Eugene took Scott into his office and agreed to loan him money to make the down payment but it was to be paid back with interest. Nothing like a loving Mormon family, loaning money to your children with interest! At least he finally opened his wallet, though only after being yelled at by a woman who he considered his inferior. I guess I won after all.

We bought our home and settled in. I had never lived in such a nice place. I really loved my home and enjoyed my neighbors. I continued to be active in the Mormon Church and made friends with the ladies in my Ward. Since I could no longer get counseling from Mary, I wanted to find someone in Chico. A new friend, Martha Longview, told me her husband Phil was a pastoral counselor with a private practice. I felt it would be wonderful to have a counselor in the Mormon Church and that he could better help me deal with my husband and kids and improve my marriage. I started private counseling with Phil and also joined his therapy group. Four other ladies from the Church were attending this group, so I felt I had a good support system with private sessions and group therapy. I tried to get my husband into marriage counseling but he refused. I even went to my ward Bishop, who managed to get Scott in for a few couples counseling sessions, but it was no use. Scott refused to continue, stating that I was the one with the problem.

We renewed friendships, especially with Scott's old girlfriend Katie Alvarez. They had been together before his missionary work, and broke up during his mission as she met and married Jose. When we returned to California, they were happily married and already had four children. We had many family events together and became good friends. Jose considered Scott as his best friend, while Katie and I enjoyed talking and having our kids play together.

Facing the darkness

I think 1988 was one of the darkest and hardest years of my life. So many things happened that year. I started to have problems with my mother. When I was around her I could not breathe and kept feeling so angry inside that I just wanted to kill her. I did not understand this at all. Why was I not able to breathe and why was there this ball of rage inside of me when I was around her? I remember once talking to her about my sex life and Scott not being interested. She kept prying for details and I became so uncomfortable that I told her I was not feeling well and had her leave the house. I was at a fabric store with her once, and kept trying to stay away from her in the store. I could not stand being next to her and felt repulsed when she would try to come over to talk... I just could not breathe and it was really hard to hide it. Later in the car with her I felt the rage swelling inside of me. All I wanted to do was pull over and kill her. This seemed insane and I could not understand these feelings at all. I thought I must be going crazy.

The situation at home was getting worse. Sometimes after Scott and I would fight, I would find myself curled up hiding under the pinball machine. He was becoming angrier and I thought of leaving, but I was scared because I had no work skills and remembered what a failure I had been living on my own prior to marriage. Scott only cheered up when we went to spend time with Jose and Katie.

At this time, I began to notice that Tory was being picked on. It was like when a flock of birds picks on one bird, continually picking at and pushing that bird around. Tory appeared to be that bird that everyone picked on. It really bothered me because I remembered being the same age and being the one every kid picked on. When I was in kindergarten and first grade, getting off the bus and walking home was an ordeal. There was always a bigger kid leading the others to tease and hit me. I used to numb myself and just walk forward, ignoring the other kids who heckled and hit me all the way home. My mother saw this but never did anything to stop them. I saw the same thing happening in my daughter and it really hurt. Why was this happening to her when I loved her and took care of her? Why was this cycle still repeating? It struck me deeply, like a voice yelling over and over inside, 'Why is this happening? You must do something about it!'

Everything was coming to a head in my life and things were about to change forever. One day a woman in my group session talked about a memory of her mother sexually molesting her. I felt very uncomfortable and thought maybe I did not belong there. I had no memories of this kind in my life. I was Mormon and those things did not happen when you are Mormon. I announced that I did not relate to this, so Phil had everyone take a break. He took me aside and told me that I had symptoms of being an incest victim. I had no idea what he was talking about – what was incest? He explained that it was when one or both parents had sex with their own child or children. I was deeply shocked at his suggestion. I had no memory of anything like that. It was impossible! I had a perfect Mormon family. I started to get dizzy and sat down to compose myself. The other women came back and saw the state I was in. I explained what Phil had said and that I did not believe him. I got no break with these ladies! They repeated that I did have signs of molest and/or incest and started telling me what they were: (1) I had no appropriate boundaries in social circles and no self-respect; (2) My thoughts and actions were extreme – I either talked too loudly, too much, too angrily, too sadly, too something; (3) I let my husband walk all over me and did not defend myself, I let my family walk all over me and was the family scapegoat; and (4) the fist fights and verbal abuse in my family from childhood to adulthood. I could hear what they were saying but was still blind to their meaning, due to my own lack of boundaries preventing me from seeing these as signs of being an incest victim. I would go from one extreme to another in my reactions. It was so hard for me to see. How could I recognize what they were talking about when I did not even know what appropriate boundaries were! What I considered functional was actually dysfunctional.

I returned home very upset. Between what was happening with my mother and not knowing how to respond to Phil's accusation of being a possible incest victim, I did not know what to think. I kept his information to myself for several days, thinking about the houses I'd lived in. I went to kindergarten and first grade when we lived in the first house, to second grade when we lived in the second house, to third and forth grade while in the third house, and fifth and sixth while in the fourth house. One thought permeated my mind. Why did I relate my life history by what grade I was in and not my age? It really bothered me that I kept track of my life by what grade I was in. When I thought about my first house again, I could remember going to school, playing Batman & Robin with plastic capes in the playground, and just a few memories of school. Why? I could not remember my teacher, what she looked like or what her name was. I could not remember my first grade teacher or what the classroom looked like. I just remembered learning to read with stories about Dick & Jane. I remembered 'good job!' stickers but that was all.

I realized I could not remember any of my birthdays, Christmas, Thanksgiving or Halloween in my first house. I did remember that I wanted to have a slumber party for my birthday but my mother said no and I was hurt. Why would a mother refuse her child a slumber party on her birthday? What was wrong with inviting girls over to spend the night? I started to shake inside. I couldn't breathe again and felt the rage welling up inside. I pushed my pillow to my face and just screamed. I screamed and screamed until I began to cry and still did not know why. I pulled myself together and envisioned my first home. I could see the house and imagined walking up to the front door. I tried to see myself walking into that first house but could not open or go past the front door. It hit me like a ton of bricks. I could not remember being "inside" the house I lived in. I barely remembered what it looked like inside. I could not remember my own bedroom. For the first time I began to see consciously the gaps (what I later called the 'black hole of suppressed memories') in my life.

I always related my life as if it were a puzzle with the pieces all tossed about. Each time I tried to put the pieces together my mother would confuse me by saying that I was remembering it wrong. Things were never how I remembered and I was always wrong. So the puzzle pieces stayed skewed. The realization that I could not remember being inside my own house put the outside edges of the puzzle that was my life and memories back together. The inside puzzle pieces lay in that black hole of suppressed memories my parents kept taking apart. For the first time, the puzzle pieces began to fit. I knew deep inside that there was no turning back for me. It was the beginning of the end.

Learning the truth

I went back to Phil in a private session and told him that I did not remember being inside my house. I told him how I could not breathe and wanted to kill my mother when I was around her. I asked him if

I was going crazy. He said not at all, and explained that what I was feeling was very normal when you have been a victim of sexual abuse. He said that not being able to breathe was probably a body memory of something that my mother did to me. Phil explained to me that I was very angry at my mother because of things she had done to me, and that I needed to understand and work through these memories in order to heal.

Phil made me feel much better, explaining again that what I was feeling was normal and not to be afraid. He asked if he could hypnotize me to help me remember and work through what I was experiencing. He told me what hypnosis was and that he was a certified hypnotherapist. He had me relax, think about my first house, and imagine walking up to the front door. As I envisioned my first house, I saw myself as a very little girl going up to the front door. The door knob was the same height as my eyes so I was about 3 years old. I opened the door and became very frightened. Sheer horror run through me and I wanted to run away. I could hear Phil's voice telling me that I was safe now and could protect myself. It was all over and these are just memories that could no longer hurt me. I had the power now and I could remember and still be safe. In my mind I opened the door and went into the front room. I began to see feet walking around me chanting. I was lying naked on the carpet in the front room and could see different feet walking in a circle around me. I did not know what they were saying, but felt I was being punished somehow. My mind took me down the hallway and I saw myself playing at the end of the hallway with my back against the wall and a big chalkboard in front of me. Phil asked me why I was playing at the end of the hallway. I said that way I could be safe if my back was to the wall and then I would know when my mom was coming to hurt me. When Phil was done with the hypnosis, I came awake crying for the little girl that had to live in the house. I could feel her as she lay on the floor, vulnerable and scared by those walking around her chanting. I felt this little girl's fear of her mother and how she had to have her back to the wall just to play. Those were my first recovered memories. They were very hard because it was the first time that I embraced what I had felt and experienced in my first house at the hands of my mother.

Phil told me that we always start with memories that are less traumatic. It is like getting in a hot shower. First we put our hand in to test the water to see if it is too hot or cold. Memory work always starts with those memories that were less abusive. I continued hypnotherapy and recalled more about my mother. I could see the little girl and realize she always had to watch my mother's faceto change. When it changed it meant it was time to get hurt and she had to hide from her. There was no warning of what was to come next. I then found myself tied naked to the kitchen table with my mom standing over me with shiny instruments. I could not accept this memory, really doubting myself and the validity of what I was remembering. This could not have happened. My family was not like that. I shared this memory in group therapy and the women told me that this is how memories work.

I think what helped me the most to get through this was the understanding that if I felt the pain, fear, horror, sensation (like I could not breathe), or smell, then it must be real. It's just like remembering good memories, like the smell of baking bread reminding you how your grandma always made bread and you remember eating the fresh bread and how good it tasted. It is the same when remembering bad memories. When I understood this concept, I made the decision to commit myself to complete recovery. I decided to go back to this scary memory and talk more about it in the group. My mother was unpredictable and would grab me out of nowhere, strip me down and tie me to the kitchen table. It was a ritual that went on everyday for years. What transpired there depended on what she wanted. The memories varied. Sometimes it was sexual assault and forcing me to have an orgasm to show her control of me. Sometimes it could be pain sessions to see how much pain I could tolerate with her "shiny objects" she got from her job at a doctor's office. I remember her telling me never cry out or she would have to start over. I would use all my energy not to cry out in pain and my whole body would sweat and shake but I would not cry out. Many times I would pass

out from the pain. If she felt th
wake me, but if she was really a
that I was a bad girl for passing
again. Once she put my broth
the doorway) up in the hallway
hang there while she vacuumed
derstand why she hung me up t
my mother's face changed.

At times she would humili
side her. They would make fun
stupid or I was bad. Jake was nc
ble by my mother. He went thr
being quite small (the arm of the couch was a bit taller than I was)
and walking down the hallway into the front room to see my mother
giving Jake an enema. I felt the terror of that sight then everything
went black in my mind. My mother was known in the family for
her enemas with bleach, hot water or whatever else she thought of. I
hated her dragging me to the bathroom to insert the hose and insist
that I hold all that liquid in my rectum.

Her mother had similar problems with enemas. My maternal
grandmother was much older, living at my sister's house, she would
give herself enemas and had a fetish with eating Ex-Lax or using sup-
positories. She would try to get any of us to go to the store to get
Ex-lax for her. We just got her Chocolate. If she did get her hands on
Ex-lax she would make a big mess in the bathroom, which was very
disgusting. My mother always felt she had to give us enemas and it
was just another thing that I had to watch out for. My mother was a
very emotionally sick person.

After doing this memory work, I talked with Phil about setting
boundaries with my mother. I decided to call and let her know that
I remembered her molesting and assaulting me since I was a small
child and didn't want to be around her for awhile. In response, she
was very calm and did not protest at all. She just agreed that if this
was what I wanted to do then it was fine with her. She seemed indif-
ferent to what I was saying. Despite her indifference, I felt hugely

.o be around her anymore. I was taking
.yself from the abusive people in my life.

.d in the church had told me about Goat Rock Beach, say-
.as very beautiful and calming. It helped you feel centered
. rejuvenated. I told Scott that we needed a family outing to this
.each. I made a picnic lunch and we had a great time there. As we
walked along the beach the tide was coming in and the waves made
huge splashes against the rocks. Scott took Mark around these rocks,
even after I told him to please be careful with Mark. Scott came back
around one of the rocks without Mark. Just then I saw a big wave
hit the rock that Mark was behind. I screamed at Scott to get Mark,
but he just stood there. I ran towards the rock to get Mark, but Scott
grabbed and held me. I was terrified that Mark had been washed
away and was drowning. I fought free of Scott and ran to the rocks
screaming for Mark. Then Mark came walking around the rocks dry
as a bone. I could not believe my eyes that he was safe and not even
wet. I held him crying over the thought that I might have lost him.
Scott just stood there without emotion. It was a miracle that Mark
was not wet or worse. The angels protected him and I cannot thank
them enough for keeping him safe. I would not let go of Mark or
Tory, and walked passed Scott giving him a look of „you pig". I went
to the car and demanded we go home. All the way home I wondered
if he had been trying to kill Mark. I never trusted Scott again and it
was the beginning of the end of our marriage.

Amy remembers our mother

During this time, my sister Amy was having emotional problems. I loved my sister and spent time at her house, just as I had
done as a teenager. When I was growing up, her children were close
to my age so they were like my sisters. I'd always enjoyed Amy, her
kids and grandkids. I noticed that lately, Amy would sit for two or

three days doing nothing. Finally she went to a counselor on her hospital medical plan to get help for her depression. Our maternal grandmother had moved into Amy's house. She was about 87 years old and the home she'd been placed in was so dirty that my sister got angry and took her home to take better care of her. I think having our grandmother in her home was the catalyst for submerged memories surfacing about our mother. This was a dangerous time for her and for me. She continued with counseling through the hospital for about six months, and was prescribed antidepressants.

Amy used letter-writing techniques to work out her memories of our mother abusing her. She believed that all she had to do was write a few letters, gain some self power, and she would be healed from childhood abuse. I wish it were that easy. I remember her telling me that it was always mom who abused her and dad never knew, that she always did it when he was working. Amy could not believe for a moment that dad had anything to do with any abuse. She was very protective of him. Looking back, her counseling was like a small patch on a leaking dam of memories. I don't think she ever finished her recovery work.

As Amy began talking about her memories of our mother I told her some of my memories and about my phone call asking her to stay away from me. Amy wanted to support me in my recovery and I wanted to support her. It all seemed to be a good thing. Then one day I told her about a memory I had of her and Jake laughing at me as I was lying on the bed naked. It was not a bad memory but I wanted to talk to her about it. She started yelling at me that she was not a child abuser and how dare I make this up about her. She continued that I was an ungrateful bitch after all she had done for me. I tried to say that she'd misunderstood, but I could get nowhere with her. She was out of control and I finally hung up. Amy was not done though and drove over to my house. She brought some clothes I'd loaned her and came to my front door demanding to come in and work this out. I answered the door asking her to please calm down, but she forced her way in yelling that she was not a child molester and we needed to get this taken care of right now. I kept telling her to calm down but

41

she would have none of it. She kept yelling and I started to stand up for myself. She then punched me in the face and I punched her back. She looked completely shocked that I would stand up for myself and had the gall to return a punch to her face. How dare I hit her but it was ok for her to hit me? I will never forget that moment. I turned away to phone the police. She came running after me and tore the phone off the wall. I told her to stop yelling and get control of herself because she was scaring my daughter (Mark was at school). All I could think of was getting Tory away from her. So I picked Tory up and left my house with Amy shouting that if I left she would never talk to me again. I went to a neighbor's house and called the police. Amy left after twenty minutes and that was the last time I spoke to my sister.

Looking back, it can be volatile to have siblings support each other in their recovery work without the skills to know that even if they did abuse each other it was not their fault. It was our parents who taught us and forced us to do this. We were the children and they were the adults. My sister was not ready to hear or accept this. She did not have the skills to support me let alone her own recovery. Nor was I ready to accept or have the skills to support her recovery along with my own. Given that my family was taught to solve problems through violence, this is exactly what my sister did.

I also had a problem accepting the fact that my father was involved with the molestation. Up until now, it was always my mother. But now I started having memories about my father. I decided it was better to be alone in recovery since my sister had been so clear about our father having nothing to do with the abuse. In Amy's mind, he knew nothing and did no wrong. Well I beg to differ. It was very hard for me to accept that my dad abused us, since my sister refused to believe that he had any part of it. In group therapy I shared a dream of being tied to the table and this time it was my dad at the end of the table. It was a very real dream and I felt confused. I lifted my head and saw my dad with his pants off. Then I saw my mother and Jake beside him. Dad was asking me if it felt good. I felt the sheer horror again, like when I first walked in the front door of my first house. I put my head down on the table, everything went black, and I woke up. I could still feel the pain and horror. I just cried, realizing that things were worse than my first memories. Shortly after that dream I had a memory in private counseling. I saw my dad naked on his bed with Jake and he was ordering Mom and Amy to hold me face down on the bathroom floor and force something up my rectum. It was a punishment for saying no to "making him happy" by sucking his penis. Then my mother gave me a very painful enema. I was continually being hit and told that I was bad for disobeying daddy. Then I heard him say "He was the stud duck around here" and I'd better do what he said. This memory was really hard and I did a lot of crying because I was such a little girl, about three or four years old and this was what I had to live with and survive. I cried for the little girl who had no protective parents.

The rage welled up inside of me at my parents. I could no longer even attempt to have any kind of relationship with my mother. I felt the warrior woman inside of me and her overwhelming strength to survive. I realized that this warrior woman was the warrior girl who defied "making daddy happy." This little girl did not care. She would fight back no matter what, and as I realized much to my detriment, was tortured by them for her defiance. But she never gave in, ever!

Scott continued making life very hard, but I was still afraid to leave him with two kids in tow. I was afraid that I could not take care of my kids or myself, and that I would be homeless. I now had no family support with my mother and sister alienated. My brother Jake was married and living in Utah and we never talked with each other. My brother Jason stopped talking to me and his wife Sally was angry at me for talking about my mother abusing me. She refused to teach Tory ballet because what I was saying was getting around the church. She thought it put a negative light on her name and that I was an embarrassment to her and Jason. As always Jason never stood up for anything except what Sally told him to stand up for.

In early 1989, my friend Katie had a baby and I was very happy for her. I noticed that the baby did not look much like her other kids. Katie was Japanese and her husband was Hispanic, while this baby had lighter hair and skin. I did not think much of it at the time, but Katie called about two months later and told me she wanted to clear her conscience. I did not understand what she was talking about. She told me that she and Scott had sex several months ago. It was a short lived affair, which she regretted and wanted to stop. Scott kept trying to convince her to keep it going despite her objections. This went on for several months and she was tired of him trying to pressure her to have sex. She had told Jose about the affair and they decided to make their marriage work. She was on shaky ground with Jose and needed to keep Scott out of the picture. Katie apologized to me and asked my forgiveness for betraying our friendship. Jose told me that if he ever saw Scott again he would beat him up for screwing his wife and calling him best friend. How dare Scott call Jose his best friend while trying to have sex with his wife? Jose told me he didn't have any ill feelings towards me and I thanked him for his honesty and ended the phone conversation.

I was stunned at this revelation and confronted Scott. He insisted that she was lying and pregnancy hormones were causing her confusion, so she did not know what she was talking about. He worked very hard to convince me. I told him that I did not want to talk to him and needed space to think about this. I kicked him out of our bedroom and locked my door at night. I was really afraid he would come to my door at night to see if I had locked it. Then I became afraid for my children because they were out there with him. I brought the children into my room and had them sleep with me.

I really thought about Scott, our marriage, and what was happening. Scott was always trying to invalidate me and I needed to see for myself what was true and what wasn't. I wanted to make clear decisions and have no doubts. Scott was very good at making me believe that I did not understand and that I was stupid. I had put up with it for nine years and I did not want to fall into that trap again. I realized that there had been a couple of incidents that had looked wrong but I had tossed it aside thinking that there was no way Scott was making passes at Katie. We were family friends and Scott would not do that to his best friend.

I decided that actions spoke louder than words and I would test him. I refused to talk to him about Katie to see what he did. Like clockwork, in two days time he began telling me this was not a big deal and wanted me to call Katie and tell her that everything was ok and we should all be friends again. I could not believe my ears! He had no remorse, no concern about my feelings, about keeping our marriage together, or about how I was hurt by his infidelity. He only wanted me to call Katie so we could all be friends again and pick up where it left off before Katie called me. I may not be the sharpest knife in the drawer but I am not the dullest either. I realized then that he had no love for me or for our children. My rebuttal was that Katie and Jose did not want him in their life ever again. You called Jose your best friend and screwed his wife behind his back. What makes you think you can have it back the way it was?! What part of reality do you live in? I then informed him that Jose made it very clear that if he sees you again around his family he will have you beaten up. Scott became unglued at the thought that he could be beaten up by Jose. Scott was not a brave man physically. He reminds me of the saying, "A coward dies a thousands deaths, a soldier dies but once." In that moment, Scott died ten thousand times. Scott was afraid of violence and the thought of Jose beating him up only showed what a true coward he really is.

This was the final straw and I became so angry at him that I no longer cared whether I would be all alone in taking care of myself and my kids or that I might be homeless. All my fears of making it on my own fell away. I remember thinking I would be better off homeless with my kids than with this man that did not love any of us. I had enough and I wanted him out right away. He blamed me and I told him to pack his clothes and get out of the house. After Scott left I felt a huge weight lift off of my back. I felt lighter and better and was not at all sad that he left. Looking back I never shed one tear for him. Some women cry when their husband leaves but I felt glad he was gone. It was nothing but a huge relief and the start of a new life.

Chapter 3. New beginnings

There I was all alone in the house with my two kids and the future in front of me. I no longer had any family support. Neither my siblings nor Amy's children ever called me to offer help or support. Scott's parents never called or tried to see the kids. We were all by ourselves.

Not long before Scott left I'd wanted to have a dog to protect me and the kids. I bought Megan, a seven-month old Rottweiler, from an excellent dog trainer with whom I formed a strong friendship that lasted many years. The kids loved Megan. One day Scott came to the house while I was gone and beat Megan so badly that I had to take her to the vet. I became afraid of what else he might try to do and decided to change the locks and garage door opener. Scott was furious, and called to threaten that if I or Jose came by his work it would be recorded on video and have both of us prosecuted. What a coward. I got a restraining order on Scott, though I was barely able to get a judge to sign it. Scott called to say how stupid I was and that I would ruin the kids if I raised them. He threatened that when Tory grew up he would get her and tell her the "truth" about me to turn her against me. He said that I would be a failure in life and not to come asking him for help. He refused to provide any financial help for the kids so I began to sell his things to put food on table.

The Bishop

Scott went to our bishop and told him some lies about why I had kicked him out of the house. The bishop felt it his responsibility to try to get us back together. He knew that I had a restraining order on Scott but decided to bring Scott over to the house anyway. He came to my door and he told me he had brought Scott over to work things out. I told him I would not let them in and had a restraining order on Scott due to his violent behavior. The bishop told me that I had no right to send Scott away and that I would be held responsible by God for ending this marriage and kicking him out. The Bishop also

46

informed me that I could not ask him to make my husband repent or make him as a Bishop take any action against Scott through the Church.

There was a part of me that shrank inside and became frightened by what God would hold me responsible for. Then the warrior woman came out again. She just rose up inside of me and I told the bishop that I did not care if Scott repented or not. It was not my problem or my responsibility. He committed adultery by screwing his best friend's wife and I made it very clear that Scott did not love me or his kids and only wanted to have Katie back. When he mentioned that God would punish me for breaking up this marriage I told him to let God punish me. I would take the stripes on my back for this marriage. I did not care if it was my fault or not.

The bishop was shocked that I stood up to him. He tried to tell me I was being misled by evil spirits and I must obey him. I told the bishop that I would not listen or obey, and that I would call the police and have Scott arrested for breaking the restraining order and he would be arrested with him. I wanted this marriage to end and to start my life over with my kids. If he could not respect my feelings and the courts of this state then he needed to leave right now. The bishop left and a couple of months later informed me that he could no longer be my bishop. I had to go to another ward and get help from the church to find another bishop. I kept wondering why the bishop was defending Scott when Scott was the one who committed adultery? Why was I the bad one?

Jason's response

During this time, I heard from my brother Jason and I will never forget that phone call. He said the Bishop had asked if he could help me with food or money for my children and he informed me that he did not like what I was saying about our parents. Then he said something very odd, that "Mom said Dad never hit me." I asked why he couldn't remember for himself if dad ever hit him. Why would mom have to tell him? I continued to ask why he was so blind to our family

47

dysfunction when he was the one with the Master's Degree in Child Psychology and Family Relations. Did he miss Denial 101 at BYU? I explained that I was the uneducated stupid one in the family, so why was I able to see the crap in our family and he couldn't see anything?

He would not respond to my questions, but said that he'd given money to the Relief Society President so she could take me to buy food. He explains that since I was not able to make good decisions in my life, that I had to go through the Relief Society President so the money would not be misused. I felt really insulted at his attitude and this statement. He said he would only help me this one time and would no longer be available to help me or my children with anything ever again. This was the brother I respected and admired as a successful person. Now he was leaving me with my life falling apart because I was trying to do the right thing for me and my kids. The family that raised me messed up my life, the in-laws were selfish snobs with their own problems, the bishop said he wouldn't call my husband to repentance for committing adultery and that I would be held responsible by God for my marriage not working. Once again the Mormon values I was taught were nowhere to be seen and the leaders only got worse as time went on.

Divorce proceedings

Scott got an attorney and we had to go to family court services. Scott's attorney approached me saying he would be glad to help me with this divorce. I said that as long as Scott paid his bills he would not be looking out for my best interests. I realized that I had to get an attorney. I had no experience outside of Morman circles, and was unsure of how to get an attory. I started asking questions and was referred to the feminist league. They referred me to an attorney. Her name was Janet and she was an excellent attorney and agreed to take my case and make Scott pay her fees. I was so relieved that I was able to get an attorney.

We were again ordered to Family Court Services and Scott was very defiant. After the meeting, the FCS representative pulled me aside and said in a roundabout way that FCS was not comfortable with Scott but had no legal ground to stop him from seeing the kids. They encouraged me be protective and report anything suspicious. They told the court that Scott could have visitation rights, with the usual split that I had them and he saw them on weekends and every other Wednesday. Child and spousal support was ordered and I was finally able to get money. Scott would come and collect the kids every other weekend and bring them back.

I started to have a bad feeling about the way my kids were behaving. When Scott dropped them off I told him that if I ever saw a mark or bruise on them I would turn him in for child abuse and nail his balls to the wall in a court of law. That was the last time he ever collected his kids. He wrote to my lawyer stating that he did not want to see his kids and be falsely accused of sexually molesting them. I was stunned at his behavior and how easily he abandoned his kids.

Eric joins the family

I started going to another ward and the bishop was a good man. He wanted to know about my parents and what was going on in my therapy. I explained how therapy was helping me and he said he'd had similar experiences when he was growing up in South America as a child in the Mormon Church. He wanted to continue to pay for my therapy and to help me get a fully-trained protection dog to keep me and my kids safe from Scott. My dog trainer had a 15-month old Rottweiler named Erich who was doing great in training and would be a good dog for me and the kids. My bishop paid for Erich with church money under "home protection." After I got Erich, Scott stopped breaking into the house. I think Erich got a chunk of him when he tried to break in. I wish I could have been a fly on the wall when that happened. Good dog, Erich!

Erich was a lifesaver not only for me but for Mark and Tory. I continued protection training with Erich and would bring my kids along. My trainer practiced a scenario where the "bad guy" would grab my kids and Erich would come running and take a huge bite on the agitation sleeve of the bad guy. I think it was very empowering for my children to see a dog protect them from a man who was the same size as their dad. They saw every weekend that Erich could take a large man down and that I could call him off and have him come back and sit at my side. Though I didn't realize it then, this was a very empowering healing experience for me, also. I got Erich to protect us and in case Scott or my family would come by and I was not able to defend myself, I knew Erich would protect me and the kids.

As time passed we went on family outings and participated in Chico Western days where each protection dog would show their skills. One of the highlights of the show was when Erich always saved Tory from the bad guy and the audience loved it. I learned to be a proficient dog handler. Erich made Mark feel safe and he began to open up and talk more. I felt that I was making a breakthrough with Mark and wanted to keep it going. Tory was also feeling safer and began to blossom. As I look back, it is amazing what a pet can do to heal your lives. Erich made us feel safe. Mark began to make huge progress in his development. With Erich at Tory's side she opened up and her love for Erich healed her self esteem and her heart. What a miracle Erich was in our lives.

A new home and first Christmas

The new bishop was very supportive and was helping some other women in group therapy with their recovery process. I thought at last I was able to get some help. My divorce came through and we had to move out of the house. Scott was required to pay me for the equity in the house we owned together and I found a duplex in Chico that was owned by a Church member. We got settled in and I arranged for childcare. One of the ladies in the ward watched the kids while I worked part time at a fast food restaurant. I put a big down payment on a new Isuzu pickup with a back seat. I love pickups and they always came in handy. I also treated myself to an antique bed and bedding, got bunk beds for the kids, washer, dryer, refrigerator –

I got all the practical things a person needs. Jason had said I was not able to make good decisions, but what did he know? I took my kids to Marine World and did some other fun things for them.

Mark began talking to me and asking questions. I was so amazed at his progress that I felt sure he could overcome his disabilities and claim his life. Mark had turned eight, which in the Mormon Church is when children are baptized. I could not have Scott baptize Mark and his Scott's father was not going to do anything for me, so I had the Bishop baptize Mark without any family support.

Our first Christmas together without Scott I will never forget. I was wrapping up presents for the kids late Christmas Eve. Tory got out of bed and saw me. I quickly pushed the wrapping materials behind me and asked her what she was doing. Her eyes opened wide when she saw all the presents, so I explained that Santa just came and I was organizing what he left (that was a close one). She believed my story and went back to bed with an "if you don't sleep, Santa may take it back!". That morning she gave me a present, which said "to Momo from Tory." I looked at her and said "Momo? Who is Momo?" We all had a big laugh and from then on I became Momo.

Phil, my therapist, referred me to a martial arts school that his family was involved in. He thought it would be a good idea for me to learn how to defend myself given the situation I was in. I joined the school and started to learn marital arts. I had no idea how much marital arts would heal me and become part of my life, even that it would become my career much later.

I began noticing someone sitting in a car outside my duplex. If I went somewhere he would follow me and otherwise he never left my house. I became paralyzed with fear at the thought that someone was watching me and why he might be there and whether he would hurt me or the kids. I felt the warrior woman rise in me and decided to go outside with a pen and paper. I went behind his car and started to write down his license plate number. It was his turn to be frightened and he peeled rubber trying to leave before I could write down his plate numbers. I never saw him again.

That was a very empowering and healing moment for me on my

51

own. I realized for the first time that "they" had something to fear from me, which was "the truth of what they do." I realized then that there were others who needed to keep my memories quiet and prevent what I was saying and doing in the church. It also made me realize that it was not just my parents involved, but others in the church too. However, at that time, I still did not know how deep it ran and how much they needed to keep me quiet. This was a very pivotal and powerful healing moment in my life.

Meeting church leaders

Not long after, some church leaders came all the way from Salt Lake City to talk to me about my memories and my brother Jason. I was asked to come to the Stake President's office and sat down with two men from Salt Lake City, the Stake President and my Bishop. I remember feeling dizzy and a little out of sorts and Ie could not see one of the men from SLC. His body was somehow blacked-out by my vision and it was like looking at a black silhouette. I thought I was losing my mind and I was a little scared.

The other man talked to me and he appeared to be very nice. I had no problem seeing him at all. He asked some questions about my memories of my mother and father and wanted to know if I believed these memories. Of course I said that I did. They wanted to know if I had any memories about my brother abusing me and whether he was involved. I explained that I did have some memories about my siblings being forced by my parents to participate. I asked why they were so interested and he explained that because Jason worked for LDS social services they needed to know if he should remain an employee. I was shocked that they would come to me. Why were my memories creating such rumblings in the higher echelons of the Mormon Church? He then asked what I would do to my brother if I were in his position. Again I wondered why I was being asked such odd questions. Were these not educated men who could make these kinds of decisions? Why was I so important? I responded that my brother was in denial about what our parents had done and asked that they please give him an opportunity to go to an independent counselor for recovery work. I felt that as long as he was in a recovery program he should be given a chance to keep his job. I also explained that if he was getting counseling from a person not affiliated with my counselor or the church then any memory work he did would validate what our parents did to us. Maybe true healing for all of us could transpire and I asked that the church support the healing of this family. During this whole conversation I could not see the other man and he never said a word. They asked me again if my brother should be fired and I said it was not my decision but theirs. I never heard from them again, but learned later that my brother did lose his job and move from the area.

Child support and referral to Sarah

Meanwhile, Scott was ordered to pay child and spousal support. He began to send letters with these checks saying that I shouldn't bite the hand that feeds me and that he wished I would die of a brain tumor. Every time he sent checks he addressed them to "the fucking child abuser" or "pay to the fucking order of Shelby the child abuser." One time the bank cashier questioned cashing these, and I becamse very angry and embarrased. I tried to explain to her that I had no control about how he wrote the checks but she would not listen to what I said. I asked for a supervisor, who in turn, was very sympathetic and she assured me I could cash these checks.

While I attended therapy, I used my good friends teenaged son to watch my kids. She assured me that hr son was very good with kids and always babysat her other children. However, Tory started to talk about seeing this boy's penis. I talked to my therapist and he said to call child protection services. I had concerns about problems with the Bishop and reporting this teenaged boy to CPS for possible child molestation. The therapist told me he would stand by me if any problems arose with the Bishop. Of course, my friend was very upset that I reported her son. I explained that her son had a problem and she needed to get help for him and her family. The boy was prosecuted

53

and I received victim witness support money for my children. One of the teachers in my son's special-education class referred me to his wife, a therapist who worked with child victims of abuse. This is how we met Sarah, and she agreed to accept the victim witness payments for my children's therapy.

The children talk about their father

It was not long before my kids started to tell Sarah about Scott sexually and physically abusing them. I was so numb by then, dealing with all the garbage from the church, the memory work, and the abandonment of my family. But this one more piece of garbage made me mad as hell! Once again I was forced to face another lie from Scott covering himself from these accusations. This began to explain why he refused to see his kids. Sarah told me to turn Scott in to Child Protective Services. I had no problem doing this!

Not only was Scott investigated but I was too. The officer leading the investigation was a good man and made me go through a lot of tests. I cooperated and supported the investigation completely. My children had to undergo a physical examination to see if they had been sexually traumatized. This was very hard for me to do to my children, but they did show signs of having been sexually assaulted. They were taken to another counselor for an independent CPS assessment. Scott was very upset and started to write threatening letters again. He did not cooperate with the investigation and was forced by the Sheriff's department to comply.

The investigating officer saw Scott for what he was and was determined to get a conviction. I had to give my journal for ink testing by the FBI to verify that I was not covering for myself. It was a thorough investigation and I earned support of the Chico Sheriff's Department to keep my children. The officer wanted Scott prosecuted, but my children were too traumatized to be used as credible witnesses in court.

After I received the Sheriff's Department backing, I took Scott back to court. Scott had stopped making child support payments to punish me for turning him in. I had my lawyer petition for automatic paycheck deductions to ensure I would get child and spousal support and to change child custody. It was hard to look at Scott in the same room with me. When the Judge asked why he'd stopped paying child support his response was pathetic. He tried to say that his accounts had been messed up but could not explain himself. He stuttered and stammered and made a fool of himself. The Judge did not buy any of it and made him write a check to me right there for the back child support. This was the first time my name was written on a check without foul language involved. The Judge ordered automatic paycheck deductions. He also ordered physical and legal custody of the children be awarded to me, and that a permanent restraining order be put on Scott. I had finally won over him! He could not stop paying child support, spousal support was increased and the restraining order would help keep me and my children safe.

A turning point

At this time I had three scenarios of truth fall into place for me to face. The first was when Scott exercised his visitation rights in the past he would take the children to my mother. What really upset me was that for years he always hated my mother and family and was very adamant about never associating with them yet when he had the children he was taking them to see my mother. My kids talked about this in therapy. I was so furious at Scott and felt so stupid that I didn't realize what he was doing and that I had to face another of his lies. Once again I was appaled at the truth of my own life and had to accept that my mother had never stopped abusing me and face that fact that this abuse went right on to my children. What made me so furious that all this had been done behind my back.

Then Mark told Sarah that my mother lived at my babysitter's house. I was shocked. Why would he say that? My babysitter had left town abruptly a few months earlier. I drove Mark to the house and he said that my mom lived there, though I knew she didn't. Then it hit me. I had to realize that this babysitter that I trusted was a will-

55

ing participant in my mother's actions and was allowing my mother access to my kids as well as the other children that she babysat. I had to face the fact that she was possibly a member, as were my parents, of the cult that hid itself within the Mormon Church. Upon reflection of time lines, I began to realize that several church members had recently moved out of the area. I could not fully believe that it was because of me and my family. They were leaving to protect themselves and not get caught up in what was falling apart and exposed. This was one of the most validating things that showed me the true extent of what I was trying to protect myself from. This also set the groundwork for facing the hard truth of how my parents never allowed me my own life and how involved the abuse really was.

Upon the recent revelations that there were more people involved, other than my family, I started to have more memories about my first house. I realized that my parents systematically abused me to force me to disassociate. I realized that not only my parents, but others were involved who participated in this type of abuse, not only with me but with other children. They would use hypnosis and train the disassociated parts to perform rituals and to keep silent about what they did. I remembered how my mom used to spin a spiral picture to induce me into a hypnotic state. She would name and train my disassociated parts. For example, she would set up scenarios like having the front door open and if the disassociated part went outside she would punish that part. By the time I was seven or eight, my mother had named and fully trained all of these parts and set-up an internal mental wall dividing off the parts that only lived inside the house and were taught never to go outside. These parts knew nothing about what went on outside the house. On the other side of this wall were those that only lived outside of the house. They went to school, to church (or at least the front door of the church), anywhere that was not connected to the abuse and involved people that my parents didn't want aware of what went on inside the houses. I've realized with this memory work, how sophisticated and involved this group really was and what my parents were a part of.

This was why my conscious memory could not go "inside" the

houses I lived in. That was the wall my mother put in place and I was not allowed on the other side. Nor was the other side allowed on my side of the wall. This also explained why she did not care when "I" did not want anything to do with her anymore. She still had control over the other side of my consciousness, which was not aware that "I" wanted nothing to do with her. All she had to do was give the appropriate signal or key word and those on the other side came out as they had been trained.

She still had power over me and cared nothing for my feelings or rights. I had a very hard time accepting this and the realization that my parents, of their own free will, traumatized all their children and forced us to disassociate and serve their perverted beliefs and actions. This was how they could 'have their cake and eat it too!' With this training in place it was assured that they would never be caught. I had to face the hard reality that my parents worshiped Satan, hid themselves within the Mormon Church, and that there were many other members who were involved even in the top SLC leadership. I could not see the man from SLC because he was also part of it. My conscious mind would not allow me to see a face that was only known to the other side.

I began talking to the 2nd counselor of the General Bishopric in SLC, who's niece had experienced similar abuses. He believed the Church was good and the leaders wanted to help people like me and his niece. I realized after awhile that his secretary was listening to our phone calls and I told him he would be shut down and told to be quiet. He tried to do the right thing in helping to protect me and other people in the church and did not believe that he was in any danger. Not much later his life was threatened. He could no longer talk to me and was afraid to do anything. He lost his position in the church. I had to accept that I was born into a cult and that my life had been used for cult member's sick religious beliefs, church member sex rings, and rituals.

Controlling mommy

My kids slowly began talking to Sarah about how Scott would teach them to "make mommy change" prior to my kicking him out of the house. This was the hardest thing for me to swallow. I learned that Scott had been taught by my dad how to make me switch to the other side. Before I was married my parents moved to Louisiana and I did not want to go. I was 19 years old and could make my own decisions, so my dad had to give control of me to someone else. He could not let me be on my own. I was given to Eugene Jennings. That is probably why I do not remember Scott asking me to marry him. My life was arranged without my consent or knowledge. I really became furious at this. I felt like a piece of meat with no rights and forced to live a lie that I knew nothing of! I had no right to my own life! Who were my parents to take my life, my rights, my choices for their continued heinous acts and religious beliefs! I had to accept that my life was a lie and that Scott, his parents, my parents, and other leaders and members were involved, and I lived right in the middle of these perpetrators. They knew and kept silent because they wanted to continue their evil practices. Why should they stop when I was expendable?

The cult did try to arrange my death. Somehow the universe protected me, knowing I could not see what they were doing. I slowly learned that the power of good is much greater than the power of darkness. I blindly stood in the light and that is where they could never go. I realized I was in a chess game and the stakes were my kids and my life. They needed me dead or under control. I realized this through a significant spiritual experience. I was driving home and felt a spiritual presence in my car. I realized that this presence was evil. I could feel him asking me to come back. Telling me to come back where I belong and stand on the other side. I really got angry, remembering myself as a child and all the pain and atrocities I went through because of this evil spirit. Then I remembered all the other children who still suffer for this evil spirit. I became so angry inside that the warrior woman came out in full force with such a great strength of spirit that I felt overwhelmed. I remember telling this evil spirit that I would NEVER go back, that everything he does and represents, what he has done to little children, is wrong. I told him that he is no match for my courage, my strength, and my will and what he stands for has no courage and no real strength. Everything he represents is nothing but empty powerless beliefs and lies for those stupid enough to believe in him. I made it very clear that I will fight him every step to my last dying breath and beyond. That spirit immediately disappeared and has never returned.

The mother inside dies

I went to Phil to talk about what I had learned from Sarah's work with my kids. I was grieving that I could not protect my kids and that there was another side of us I did not know that had allowed my kids to be hurt. The other side did not know I had children and that they were a part of us. This truth was very hard and I remember the mother inside that loved Mark and Tory beyond belief. She could not face the fact that she could not protect her children. It was too much for her to bear. She cried and cried in therapy, while Phil told her she had to face it and forced her to have more information than she could bear. She could no longer take this grief and she died inside. The knowledge of the truth was too much and she could not take it. I still cry for her as I write these words. It is a very real loss. When she died inside, it felt like our inner core's door opened and she went through and the door closed behind her, never to be seen or felt again.

Not long after her death the walls my mother and father worked so hard to put in place began to fall apart inside our mind. I started to have co-consciousness with the other side. One was very strong and she was in charge on the other side. The information she shared was that no one was calling them and they did not understand why. She thought that this could be the opportunity the other side wanted to get away from the mother and father. The other side hated what they were forced to do and endure and had always wanted to

59

get away but did not know how. Now that my perpetrators did not have control over me, the training my mother had put in place began to tear apart. The walls fell apart and the two sides started to become one. The strong one from the other side saw the danger I was in and what was going on and she began to share the information I needed to protect me and my kids and claim our life forever.

Questioning my beliefs

I began to question what I had been taught by the Mormon Church as the true teaching of God. How could a Church claim to be the only true church of God, being run to this day by Jesus Christ himself through the Prophet and President of the Mormon Church? How can Christ say that he runs this church yet have his appointed leaders blind to or harbor such evil people? When I asked this I was told we all have the right to choose so "just pray and read your scriptures." I hated to be told to pray and read my scriptures. I always felt like I was being invalidated and patronized. "Just shut up and don't bother me" would have been more honest.

I tried to talk to other church leaders about my thoughts but it was always the same. Just pray and read your scriptures. Well, I was not buying that and I began to realize that if this was Christ's own Church then he was not what he says he is. If this was his church then where was his responsibility to protect the good members from these evil people? Where were our rights to choose not to be victims, our rights to protect ourselves and our children from these evil people? Any leader of any church or organization, including Jesus/God, turning a blind eye makes them as guilty as those who commit these crimes. My only conclusion was that either Christ willingly allowed good people to be victims of the heinous acts of evil people or this was not Christ's only true church. In my heart I could not believe that a Higher Being, representing all goodness, would turn a blind eye in a church that He is responsible for. The only conclusion I could come to was that this was not Jesus Christ's only true church on this earth.

A church leader I felt I could trust came to my home to talk about the validity of the Mormon Church and I realized he had been talking to someone in my family. He tried to use a key word to make the other side come out so that he could control me. I became very dizzy and fought it off, holding myself together with every ounce of strength I had. When I had composed myself I realized what he had done. I asked if he had learned that from my brother or mother, but he would not say a word. Once again, a leader in the Church was violating my rights. I made him leave my home, with Erich at my side insuring his departure. This was a bold attempt to get control of me and was the beginning of the end of my association with the Mormon Church.

This church was full of lies and protects those members who are pedophiles, participate in sex rings and worship Satan. My life was a lie, sheltered in an organization that harbored and kept these people safe. Why? Because good religious people are the easiest to convince by saying "I am a man of God and it is "God's Word." These good people will blindly follow. As long as the members stay ignorant, these perpetrators thrive. The truth could not be told and I was in a volatile situation. If something happened to me my kids would go back to Scott and the cycle of abuse would continue. My daughter would go through the same training I was forced to endure and my son would be put away in a psychiatric facility. My thoughts were "Fuck this church!" If I was going to Hell for protecting myself and my kids from abusive parents and turning my back on the Mormon Church, then I already knew my way around. I was raised in the Mormon Church and my life had been nothing but Hell. I lived in hell growing up and I might go to hell when I died. At least right now I could free myself from this crap and protect my kids. Let the chips fall where they may regarding the "True Church of God," and the damnation I was destined to receive.

I was so enrage at the betrayal of the Mormon Church, the Mormon Jesus that I truly believed in, and the hell that I am destined to go to for no longer believing in the Church's blind teachings, I did not care that I was going to Hell, and when I got to Hell, Hell was going to have it's hands full with me. I will fight them every step of the way. Why? Because what they do to children is wrong and what they represent is wrong and they have no right to take children and abuse them for their heinous beliefs. I have had enough of the Mormon spiritual bullshit, toxic shame, and everything that goes with it. I could no longer stand and say this was the true church of god.

The end with the Mormon Church

I lost the bishop who had been so supportive of me. He kept getting sick and later I realized that he and his family were being threatened for helping me. He moved to another state and I had to start all over again with another bishop. The new bishop was not very supportive and did not like paying for my therapy or for childcare while I worked part time. He did not like me receiving church food or having the church help pay my bills. One day he called me into his office and said he'd had a very interesting conversation with Scott. Scott told him that I was a liar, a manipulator, and that I was the reason why my marriage did not work. I had never told him about Scott, nor given him permission to talk about my personal situation with him. I felt very violated that he was breaking confidence and speaking to my ex-husband. Once again I was being treated like a criminal and decisions were being made about me that I knew nothing about.

The bishop told me I had to put my son in a psychiatric facility, give my daughter to Scott, and go back to work fulltime if I wanted any help from the Church. I was stunned that he expected me to give up my children because that is what Scott wanted and he supported Scott over me! I told him that he had no right to do that to me. I was not the one who committed adultery, or called Jose my best friend while screwing his wife, or the one putting bruises on my children, or being investigated by the Sheriff's department for child abuse. I was in good standing with the church and he had no right to ask me to do this. He would not listen and told me that I was a liar and had to give up my kids if the church was going to support me.

I left his office and made an appointment with the Stake President, The Stake President told me I had six months to get on my feet and pay my own bills. After that the Church would no longer help me. I could not believe my ears. I needed clarification. I asked him the folloing: I asked him whether if I needed food for my kids he would help me. He said no. I asked if I was homeless and on the streets with my kids would he help me. He said no. I asked him if I was standing in the rain and he drove by would he help me. He said no. I looked at this stupid man and very facetiously told him that he was right. I remember in the Bible that Christ taught us to kick single mothers with kids to the streets. Christ taught us to keep kids hungry and homeless. Christ taught us to turn our backs on those in need. Christ taught us to force mothers to give up their children so that you would not have to help them. His response was silence. I became very angry and told him that if he would not help me he could start not helping me immediately! I walked out of the Mormon Church and never returned. Their attempt to stop all support was so I would fall on my face and be forced back to my family. Well, I did not fall on my face and I did not go back to my family. They were wrong about me, very wrong.

Chapter 4. All alone

I remember driving home realizing that I had no one to go to. The church I was raised in my whole life turned its back on me. I was always taught that the Mormon Church always takes care of its own no matter what. I guess I was not a part of the "no matter what." How dare I try to protect myself from abusive parents? How dare I protect my children and do what is right for them?! For the first time I felt all alone. I had no one to go to. I felt myself sinking inside and realized I had to sink or start swimming to survive. I will never forget that moment of truth. I started to swim. I did not know how to swim but I was going to swim.

I needed to work full time but could not with my son. Then school informed me that they could not meet the needs of my son and told me about a fulltime program for him. I went to see the people who ran this program and was recommended to put Mark in fulltime care. This meant that Mark would go to a live-in care home with other children where they would help him. They would take him to school, and provide counseling and specialized classes. It was a fully contained program that met his needs. Mark was still a handful and I saw that Tory was getting put on the back burner because of Mark. I saw that the house Mark would stay in was very clean and the people were nice.

I had a long think before I made my decision. I was afraid for Mark but knew he needed more professional help. I decided to put Mark in their program. I would check up on him without notifying anyone and saw that he was well taken care of. I went to his school and saw that they were doing a great job with him. I saw that this was a great program for Mark and they were helping him. This helped me to spend more time with Tory and work fulltime and pay my own bills. I found a way to swim and survive without giving up my kids or compromising the care my son needed.

New memories with Sarah

I began to see that my counselor was enmeshing his professional and personal life. He started having private sessions in his home and his wife, who was also a victim of ritual abuse, became more involved. I could accept having group therapy at his home to a point, but I saw that his wife was listening in on private counseling. I noticed that Phil was taking personal action against the cult within the Mormon Church. With the knowledge shared by the other side I began to see that he was being used by cult members. I think he believed he was doing the right thing, but was not clever enough to realize that he was being played. I began to see that he did not have very good boundaries and I was outgrowing his skill level of counseling. He got me started in the right direction but his personal issues were getting in the way. Since I could not afford him without the church supporting me, I decided to stop attending sessions and group therapy.

I asked Sarah if she would take my victim witness money as payment for counseling. She agreed and I started to see her once a week. With her seeing both Tory and Mark, I was able to work on re-parenting myself so I could be a better mother and help my kids and recover from the atrocities of my life in the Mormon Church. She was the one who walked with me through all my heaviest memories.

With the other side sharing information, many things came together for me regarding my life inside the houses I lived in. I will not share all of it. Many memories are so heinous that they will stay between me and Sarah. What I will share are the memories that in some way slipped over to my conscious mind and made me think I was crazy for thinking such things. As I remembered, I realized that for years the truth was staring at me and these memories became the validation I needed.

I began to realize that when our cat had kittens I could not remember what happened to them. Usually when a cat has kittens you sell or give them away, but I realized that these babies were not sold or given away. I remember her having kittens but not what happened to them. I found that odd and I had a memories of newborn kittens

65

in a box with a light bulb over it.

Then the other side shared what happened to those kittens under the light bulb. The bulb fell into the box and my mother got very angry and told me it was my fault. She made me take the crying newborn kittens and flush them down the toilet. She told me that the light had ruined them and I had to kill them. I was about four years old and did not understand why I had to kill them while they were still alive.

My father hosted sex rings for other members, and Jake and I were passed around to perform sex acts on them or had to have sex with each other. My father was obsessed with these. They made him feel powerful and he had them all the time. When people were finished with the sex sessions some would stay behind. This was the time to make sure I did not tell what happened. My mother would take one kitten at a time, cut off its head, and ask me if I was going to tell. I would say no, crying for the kittens. She would take another one and cut its head off and ask me again whether I would tell. I said no, begging my mom to stop killing the kittens. She kept going, ignoring my pleas until all the kittens heads were cut off. I was hysterical because I had promised not to tell but my mother had to make sure I understood what would happen to me if I told. I would take the kitten's heads and put them back together with the body and pray for them to go in peace. I was about three years old when this started. My parents thought me crazy for picking up the kittens and trying to make them feel better and sending them to Jesus in peace. As I look back at this I was not crazy, they were. It was acceptable for them to kill kittens, while I tried to find a way in my mind to deal with their actions if I told. I felt responsible for the kittens and all I could do was love them and give them back to God.

Growing up I always hated dogs. I never wanted to be around them and could not touch them. I do not know what made me get a dog as an adult, except that I could see that a dog could protect me and my kids. I found a way past my fear and hatred of dogs and got Megan and Erich. I never understood why I hated dogs so much until I had a memory of one of my father's sex rings. Someone brought in a German Shepherd and they put smelly oil on my bottom. The dog would mount me and they forced me to stay still while the dog humped me. It was funny for them to watch me being forced to have sex with a dog. I was teased and humiliated while this happened.

I also feared and hated snakes. My father had a box of water or garter snakes. He used them to punish me by putting snakes in my anus or vagina. Sometimes I would be punished by being locked in a box after he had thrown snakes in with me. I always had a fear throughout my childhood, teens and adulthood that a snake would come out of my bottom and bite me. I thought I was crazy for thinking such things, till I finally realized in memory work where that came from. I was about three years old and my mother told me that if I told anyone what they were doing, a snake would come out of my bottom and bite me so that I would be poisoned and die. To enforce this, she killed a snake, fried it in a pan and had me swallow it whole. I almost choked to death and after I recovered from eating the snake she told me that it would stay in my stomach and if I told anyone what they did the snake would come out and bite me and I would die.

I began to remember some satanic rituals. I realized where the rituals took place and why I was always taken to the house of the old man in charge at the Church. I always wanted to be outside that house and play while my parents were there. Because I had spiritual gifts and was able to survive what they did to me it made my father look good. They used my gifts for their religious practices.

Then the old man died and I remembered thinking it would all stop. I was really happy and told my mom that you will have to stop hurting me now that the old man is dead. I felt such relief and believed it would all stop with my reasoning of a little girl of six years. It did not stop. I discovered that my father replaced the old man and it became worse. I remember the horror of watching things start all over again and realizing that it would not stop.

My father was out of control. He became powerful, which fueled his needy low self-esteem. He was the man in charge. From six to ten years of age I really have no memory of my life. I have small pieces of rituals, clowns, goat heads and other people hurting me.

I have memories of being possessed as part of the rituals, but I do not know much. It was very traumatic and I may never remember. When I moved into our second house, it was done in the garage and became worse.

I just know that my ability to survive and spiritual gifts made my father powerful. I do not know how long it lasted or what transpired when he was no longer in charge in the Bay Area. I just remember being happy and then realizing that it was still not going to stop. A part of me died inside. That part of me went through the door to my inner soul and the door shut and that part has never been seen since. I was crushed to realize that it was not going to stop.

My father had a real need to make sure that everyone knew he was the one in charge. If I tried to stand up to him he would have me punished by my mom and siblings. His favorite punishment was to hang me in the garage by my neck. He would put this "scratchy rope" around my neck and then hit me telling me "he was the stud duck around here and I better recognize it." I would be ridiculed by the others. Then he would take me down to make sure I would not die. I remember going to first grade and looking in our bathroom mirror and wondering where the sores around my neck came from. I was so torn apart that I had no memory of what my dad had done the night before. I had to wear a turtleneck sweater to school in the spring when it was too hot for warm clothes. My mother forced me to wear it so no one would know about my neck being bloodied and scabbed from the rope.

I had to face so many things that had been bottled up inside of me. I spent many years crying to Sarah as the memories were released. I had to process all these memories and accept that I was never allowed to have my life. I had grown up with no boundaries and no self esteem and had to learn how to make better decisions to manage my fractured life.

I was all alone with no clue about how to live my life or which direction to go. My personality was either very strong, "putting all my spades on the table" or with absolutely no boundaries so that you could walk all over me. I went from one extreme to the other. It was very hard for me to see this and learn about a middle ground of choices for managing my life. My soul felt very empty and needy. I did not know what love was but I wanted to be loved. I really wanted to make friends and belong somewhere. I had no one in my life and I hated being alone. To my detriment I made friends with people who were just as dysfunctional as I was. I remember talking to Sarah about this and the theory of attraction. I spent a long time contemplating this theory and how I was attracting myself to the same kind of people I was raised with. The theory of attraction was my guide to how well I was managing my life, by the friends I had and the choices I made. I would look at the dynamics of the friends I had. Were these dynamics healthy or dysfunctional? One thing that hindered me in this was that I had an open trusting mind towards everyone and blindly believed that they were honest with me. I learned life's good and bad lessons by the choices I made.

Martial arts lifestyle

My martial arts instructors soon became a big influence in my life. Jerrod and Angela invited many students over to their house and I became one of the students that spent a lot of time with them. Tory became best friends with his daughter Mary. We went on many outings and I enjoyed spending time with them. For the first time in my life I was living and interacting with people who were not Mormons. It felt very different because there were so many people with so many different value systems and people were comfortable with that. It was strange to see people who lived their lives not according to Mormon values. I was learning about other people, other values and other lifestyles. It was very eye-opening for me to see so many people living without a church dictating their lives. It was very foreign to me not having a church with strict rigid rules ready to send me to Hell if I did not obey.

I was very innocent and did not know that people had their issues and would talk about me when I talked to them in confidence. Nor did I realize that the majority of people did not live the life I was forced to live and had no concept of such abuse. When I started going to martial arts classes, I confided in my instructor Jerrod and his girlfriend Angela about my background and the multiplicity. I did not realize until later that they did not maintain confidentiality and talked about me and my "problems" to everyone in the school. Even my housemate Sasha, when she first planned to rent a room from me, was 'warned' about me by Angela. Though I did not realize it at first, my new instructors did not have good boundaries and confidentiality was not something they did.

Our martial arts instructor was a charismatic man. He had a lot of talent but his greatest weakness was the way he loved getting attention from the ladies in his school. I began to notice that Jerrod was taking women into his office during class time and spending a long time with them when the door was closed. I remember visiting Jerrod's house and one of his lady blackbelts was sitting beside him on the couch. What felt wrong was that it was July and they had a blanket over them from the waist down, while Angela sat across from them not caring a bit. I thought it odd but said nothing. This student had only tested twice for her 2nd degree blackbelt and was promoted quickly. I never respected her rank, considering that she "schmoozed him" on the side.

I saw that I had a talent for martial arts and loved sparring. My first tournament was in August 1990 and was the last open tournament hosted by our Grandmaster. In my first sparring competition, I went up against two different women who were bigger than me. They did Ti Kwan Do and had a lot of kicks, while I was still a white belt and did not do much kicking. However, I worked my hands like a boxer, not yet understanding the difference between sparring and fighting. These ladies did not know what to do with my aggressive style. I kept blocking their kicks and stepping in to punch them. By my second competitor, I was disqualified for being too aggressive. I did not realize that in competition I was not supposed to hurt people, and I had been beating the shit out of them. I knew how to fight, but I did not understand that most people did not have the same level of violence inside them that I did. I will never forget the look on my instructor's face. He was shocked to see what came out of me in sparring. I did not want to be a person who hurt other people, so I vowed not to spar until I learned self-control.

Choosing friends and 'family'

I had to move out of the duplex due to the Mormon owner giving me too many problems. I already had a housemate, Sasha, who I'd met through the martial arts school, so we moved into a house in Chico. She was about nine years younger than me and stayed in my house for about two years. She loved to travel and did just that every chance she got, while she worked on her degree in International Relations. Sasha was not very kid-oriented but she tolerated my kids quite well. She was a free spirit and there were many times that we talked about parents and life. I would share with her the things I was learning in therapy and Sasha was very good for me. She had a completely different view on life. We were opposites in how we perceived people. I always based my opinions on honor, honesty and integrity, while she was much more cynical. We had many conversations on right and wrong versus life's choices. I was very black and white in my thinking, while she would always play devil's advocate and point out to me the many grey areas in life where choices involve many additional factors. For example, I viewed Jerrod as not being honorable in his infidelities. He had a commitment to Angela, yet he crossed the line by making passes at other women. His boundaries were not good and he crossed many lines in his private and public life. Sasha acknowledged that his actions were dishonorable, but rebutted by asking why he should stop, if Angela put up with his infidelities and the other ladies allow or even encourage him to make passes. He is having his cake and eating it, without having to suffer any consequences. So what incentive does he have to stop? I could only say because there is no integrity in is his actions and what he puts out will come back to him. Sasha taught me many ways to perceive and to use critical thinking skills. Sasha is a very intelligent woman and we have always stood by each other, through good and bad times and no matter where she is in the world. She was the first in my new 'chosen' family. You never know what the universe brings, but the universe brought me my sister Sasha.

While I was working in a fast food restaurant, I made friends with a young black man named Tyrese. He had his problems and his family had its problems. I became good friends with his ex-wife Tamika and her two young sons. I had never been around people of color. My father was very prejudiced and I did not know anything about black folks. I had no exposure at all to any people of color except my cousin who was raised on the Indian Reservation. As I spent time with Tamika, I began to see that she was just like me. I learned that people of color were just as human as I was. They had the same feelings, hopes, dreams, disappointments, laughter, love, anger, humor and most of all a spirited love for life. Her kids were just like mine. They went through the same developmental stages as any other child. I am sad to say that I was very naive and had no knowledge of anyone but Mormons.

I can truly say that African-Americans played a big role in healing my life. I had many African-Americans come into my life and made friends with all of them. I did not go out looking for them. The universe brought them to me. It was an eye-opening experience. People of color became human to me and I am very glad my eyes were opened to see such beautiful people. I was able to talk to Tamika about my life and she did not mind hearing about it. I really enjoyed her friendship and spending time with her and her sons.

I made friends with an African-American man named Tom who was training in my martial arts school. He did not want a relationship but we were good friends. No longer being held to the value system of a church of lies, I decided to have an affair with him. I wanted to free myself from the guilt and make my own decisions about my life and my body. I chose to claim my rights as an adult to enjoy my own body. I had my life and he had his and there was no commitment to each other. Sasha watched Tory for the nights that I would go to his house. We drank wine and he taught me that sex was something wonderful. I learned to share that with him. I realized that I was not going to hell and that I had a right to make adult decisions and still be a wonderful person. All the Mormon teachings that kept control of me were falling apart. It was very empowering for me to make my own choices without any religious Hell hanging over my head. My affair only lasted about two years, but I cannot thank Tom enough for showing me how beautiful sex is and that it is OK to share.

CHAPTER 5. EMPOWERMENT

My empowerment took many avenues. I saw that there were many people who knew nothing about the life I was forced to live. I realized that my abusers had more to hide than I did, because the rest of the world did not live like them. This concept was very empowering to me. My abusers had weaknesses and things to hide from the outside world. They became vulnerable in my eyes and I became stronger.

The other side that had never lived in the outside world marveled at many things. I will never forget one day when I took Tory to the playground. The other side saw many children playing and their parents playing with them or watching them. They were shocked to see happy children. For the first time, they saw how these children were free to play, free to speak, free to cry, free to express anything and not be punished. I began to cry realizing the difference between what I'd had to live through and how other people lived free from this abuse. These moments were very powerful. The more I lived and experienced life the more I learned and grew. It was a very hard time to live through, surviving paycheck to paycheck, not always having money and making mistakes with my bookkeeping. I learned the hard way how to manage money, but I learned with the help of my new friends.

My family wants me back

One day at the fast food restaurant, one of my sister's daughter come in wanting to talk to me. It had been almost two years since I had walked away from my family and about eight months since I had walked away from the Mormon Church. Now my niece walked into my job, though I had never told any family member where I worked. Though I was offended that she had come and knew where I worked, I took a break and went over to talk to her. She told me that my family loved and missed me and wanted me to come back. I just looked at her and saw that she was a little disoriented. She was like a robot doing what she was told to do. For the first time I was able to see

74

clearly the signs of the trauma inflicted on me by my mother and father in another family member. It was very validating that I was going in the right direction with my life.

I listened to her ask me to come back to the family and how much they loved me. I started to get really angry about the hypocrisy of what appeared to be an honest but shallow show of concern for me. I told her that my family did not love me or they would have called to ask if I needed anything when my children had no food. They would have offered me help when I needed a place to live. Where were the phone calls when my life fell apart and my husband left me to get a divorce? Why I was only allowed a one-time offer from Jason and told there would be nothing else? I told her that she had not once called to see how I was doing, so why was she here after almost two years asking me to come back?

I told her that I remembered what mom and dad did to me and I knew what mom did to my kids. I told her to tell my mom that if I ever saw her again private or public I would beat her ass! I did not care if she took me to court and sued me for assault. I would be glad to go to court and talk about what she did to my kids. We would see what the judge had to say. If I see my mother ever again I will beat her so badly she will need rehabilitation for the rest of her life no matter how old she is. My niece just sat there as if she did not hear a word I said. Without any emotion on her face, like a robot, she said OK and got up and left. A couple of weeks later I got a letter from my sister. She had written the right street but the house number was wrong. I was offended again that they knew where I lived though I had never given them my address. Her letter said that I had better come back to the family and "maybe all might be forgiven." She said that I was a terrible person for not appreciating all she had done for me and telling lies about her. So I was ungrateful and bad for telling lies but "all might be forgiven" if I came back? I just filed the letter away and never responded, because I did not need to be forgiven for protecting myself and my children.

I learned that silence was my best protector. I realized then that they would always know where I was. I was angry that they kept

75

making the effort to find out where I lived, but I decided that it did not matter. They might know where I am but they would never cross the line by coming in. I felt that if they came into my home I would just unleash my anger and kill them. I was not going to live in fear of them and if they knew, then they knew. I was going to live my life anyway and I decided that they had no power over me and I was not going to give my power to them. They had more to hide and were not willing to expose themselves. Sarah taught me "I am not responsible for your actions, but I am for mine." So I took responsibility for my actions. I had to take care of me and my kids and always use safety rules to protect all of us. I no longer cared if they knew where I was or what I was doing. They could not get their hands on me and they could not control me. I had my life and I planned on keeping it.

Boundaries and job skills

I still did not have good boundaries. I spent most of my time in therapy talking about life skills and what I was experiencing. I remember once at a pet shop I started talking to a complete stranger. She was very kind and listened to me as I talked about my abuses. I remember hearing myself talking and thinking that I needed to shut up because I did not know this person. I finally got hold of myself and politely went home. Talking about this with Sarah I started to see that I needed better boundaries with people I interacted with. I needed to learn how to shut up.

I needed to re-parent myself. It was very hard to see my own faults and to face my mistakes. As always I grabbed the bull by the horns and tried to wrestle it down. My personality was very strong and up front and I usually turned people away from me. My fast food job went well and I learned through my mistakes. A lady there took me under her wing and told me that I was very intelligent and should get a better job. I had learned medical insurance billing from my mom when I was eighteen and had a couple of jobs in doctors' offices and hospitals. However, it had been several years since I had worked and when I interviewed I was treated as if I was ignorant because I did not have "current" experience.

On one interview the manager was particularly patronizing, telling me that I would have to answer phones and use a calculator. I got so angry, knowing I would not get the job, that I politely told her that she was right, the way we answer phones had changed since I last worked. You had to pick up the phone and say "Hello, Dr So and So's office. How may I help you?" I facetiously told her you would not be able to train me to use a phone by putting in a series of numbers to reach a certain person. I just got up and walked out the door with that woman's mouth wide open. To this day I really hate empowered dysfunctional management and decision making.

I was working part-time graveyard shift as a guard with Erich. One night a man came into the scrap metal yard we were guarding and tried to steal radiators. As I was doing my rounds I saw this man frozen in a running stance. I called for Erich to come and 'Watch him!' That was his signal to be alert and ready to protect. The man ran and Erich took off after him. He ran up a metal bin next to the fence and jumped up to grab the tree and climb over the fence. Erich jumped up after him and missed biting his ankle by less than an inch. The guy was bold and came back later. Erich chased him and just missed him again as he went over the fence. By the time I got home it really hit me, "what if he'd had a gun?" It shook me up and I realized that I needed to put myself in better work situations that did not put my life in danger.

I decided to lie on my résumé that I worked in Arizona and just moved to the area. Within a week I was hired to do radiology billing. It did not take me long to understand the system and I became very proficient. My boss was one of the best I have ever had and she worked with me to improve my professionalism and office conduct. I had to tone down my strong personality in the office and learn to work with others and their differences. I spent a lot of time talking to Sarah and learning how to find a medium ground for dealing with things. One of the things that permeated every level of my being and life, was that "I respect myself too much to allow you to treat me like this." I respected myself and expecting others to do just that.

Martial arts development

I loved martial arts and was developing my skills. A new student, Aaron, who'd gotten his blackbelt in Korea while in the Air Force, had joined the school. His wife Annie was also a blackbelt and they had two daughters and a son. I saw that Aaron was proficient in sparring and decided to learn from him. Jerrod's talent was flashy forms and techniques rather than sparring. Aaron taught classes sometimes and I made sure to attend. I loved how he taught sparring and I began to learn how to control my anger and spar rather than brawl. It was very difficult to learn, because the size of the fight in me was huge. It was like asking a charging bull to please gallop with grace. I am still learning how to gallop with grace.

Most of the women in my martial arts style were not fighters and I won tournament sparring in my division every year. There were always ladies who had a hard time with me and even years later as a blackbelt I still had to tone my sparring down. One year I thought I was using good control, but the lady I was sparring was getting upset. The Grandmaster came and shook his finger, telling me to use better control or I would be eliminated. I was shocked and hurt, thinking I was already exercising good control! A friend who was helping judge told the center judge that actually I was being more controlled than normal. The judge looked shocked. I worked hard to make friends with the ladies afterwards, to show that I was not a rude person. I am still friends with two of these ladies and we laugh about my early reputation.

There was one instructor in California who did appreciate my sparring style. He had been a champion fighter in Europe and was knighted by the Queen of England. He loved the fact that I could "sling them things." His forte was sparring and I realized we were kindred spirits. We both had raging bulls in our souls. He has watched my development and we have become good friends.

John, a 3rd degree blackbelt who had known Aaron since they trained in Korea together while in the Air Force, came to stay with Aaron and his family. He was going through a difficult separation from his wife and Aaron offered him a place till he could sort things out. He made friends with everybody and I really developed a crush on him. I tried successfully to get his attention. We became close and were lovers for a short time. He also liked a Korean lady in our school, named Kay, who reminded him of his ex-wife. She was married but he kept flirting with her.

Finally, John decided to go back to Arizona to work things out with his wife. I was really crushed that he left. I loved him and wanted him in my life. Before he left he lied to Kay about me, saying he had not invited me to her house for dinner with the Grandmaster, while telling me that Kay had invited me. Kay was a very proud woman and I lost her friendship because of this. John had many personal issues and in the long run it was better that I did not stay with him. I heard about him from time to time, but it was always the same. He was having problems and could not get his life right. He has always continued from one problem to another and has never found happiness.

I enjoyed my training and considered it important to my life. Everyone knew that our instructor liked the ladies. I would watch him develop closer relationships with certain women, who always got promoted a little faster than the others. I never respected these women who were promoted rapidly and politely ignored them. In our style you had to earn your blackbelt. You tested every three months, and usually for a minimum of 6 to 8 tests before receiving your 1st degree blackbelt. The higher your rank the more you were tested for the next rank. Jerrod usually promoted the first degree candidates in 4 to 6 tests. I watched Jerrod get promoted to 2nd, 3rd and 4th degree blackbelt and his ego became bigger with every promotion. Teaching quality started to diminish as the years passed. Lazy was the word that best fit.

Jerrod made the rounds to all the ladies in the school and my turn came. He started flirting more seriously at around the time I was starting to test for my blackbelt. I had spent a lot of time with his family and looked up to and cared for him very much. Still, I was not comfortable with his behavior towards me when I was friends with

Angela. I had to decide what to do, as I was testing for blackbelt and did not want my training to stop. I loved martial arts and was fearful that he would snub me.

After talking to Sarah about it, I realized that Jerrod did not take responsibility for his actions. He was a sex addict and in his element by having so many ladies swooning over him. It was easier for him to make advances and let a situation fall into place. Then he could easily point the finger at the woman as instigator and take no responsibility for his own behavior. I was not going to accept this. True to my spirit I decided to handle him directly. I invited him to lunch and we went to pizza. After eating and chatting I told him that I had one more thing to talk to him about. He was obviously curious about what I was going to say. I told him that he has been "knocking on my door" for sex and explained that if he kept knocking he would get exactly what he asked for. I had no commitment to anyone and if he kept it up he would get it. His mouth hit the ground. He could not believe how bold I was, putting complete responsibility for his actions back in his lap.

Taking responsibilities for his own actions was not something he was comfortable with. He could not kick me out of the school because I had done nothing wrong. I had simply put my spades on the table and allowed him to make his own decisions. He left me alone after that. He also stopped teaching me. I only told Sasha and unless he discussed it no one else in the school knew what had happened between us. I decided to kill him with kindness after that. I loved my martial arts training and was not going to allow him to stop me. So I kept training and a year later was still testing for my blackbelt. The other students began to question why I was not getting promoted.

Spiritual matters

I started going to a black Baptist Church with Tamika. I had never been to another church, except with my aunt (my dad's sister) when we visited them. I remember going to the church and seeing a band with drums, guitar, tambourines, and electric piano. I had never have seen such things in a church before. They played "bumpin" music with lots of soul. I was shocked to hear such great music. I loved it. I did not know that a church could play such great music during services. My old church was boring in comparison. The Minister was a very intelligent, well-educated man. I spent time talking to him about my life and my spiritual questions. He told me that the reason I felt so comfortable with black folks was because of the hard struggles I had in life. He told me how black folks struggle and the similarities.

I began to see how black folks were discriminated against and the huge differences between the "white" and the "black" point of view. Maybe one day our country will humanize all people of color and no longer see color/religion as different, or "not like us" but rather see all people as being "a part of us." We are all related.

It really amazed me how he talked about Jesus and that he really believed that with Jesus you can accomplish anything. It was like a breath of fresh air. The difference between the Mormon leaders and his counsel was like night and day. I decided to be baptized by him. It was a very moving experience and I could feel the angels around me. I really started to struggle with myself about spirituality and what was true and what false. I wanted to understand Christianity and felt I needed to stay within that group or "I would go to hell," but I felt a different spiritual pull. I felt strongly pulled to Native American beliefs and practices, though I could not understand this at all. My cousin was raised on the reservation but my parents denied any native blood in my veins. I remember being about five and had just learned how to swim underwater. My brothers went off to shoot some frogs and made me promise not to swim. Of course I started to swim and at some point I started sinking. I remember a native man pulling me out of the water. He asked me where I lived and I pointed up to the cabin. I remember not wanting to tell him and wanting him to take me to his house. I could not ask him to save me from them so he took me to my parents.

I always felt a native spiritual presence around me growing up. I do not understand why but I always felt him near me. I also felt my Great Grandmother on my father's side. She died before I was born but I could always feel her around me. I just put it to my being weird. I was strongly attracted to native and new age/pagans beliefs. When I went to the Baptist Church I knew it was a good church and the Minister believed in the words of Jesus. I saw that I had to decide which spiritual direction I wanted to walk down. I always felt better when I went to Pow Wow's and felt "at home." I did not know anyone but I could feel peace inside me. It felt like "me," but I did not belong. I would struggle with this for many years, trying to understand why. Finally, I decided I could no longer be part of any Christian church due to the events of my life. I could not re-create the same environment I grew up in. I decided to walk a native path.

Leo

I was still friends with Tyrese and became friends with his mother Paula and her husband Leo. I quickly saw that Paula loved to have drama in her life. She was addicted to prescription pain pills and I often saw her high on pills as she stumbled around her house. She was a person who did not feel alive unless she had someone to fight with. She was either suing her employers after falling down on a sidewalk or was a raging terror to anyone else so she could feel justified in her life. If she did not have a volatile situation going on she did not know how to live. Drama defined her life and made her feel better about herself. She also had a real need to bring others down so that she could feel better. Much later I realized she was dangerously crazy.

Leo was easier going, though he did not appear to be a happy person. I remember looking at him once and I could see his soul. It was a like a caged lion pacing back and forth, hating where he was and wanting to be free. There was something about Leo that attracted me. I could feel his soul and see that he was a good man. At the same time he was not someone to take lightly and had no problem in "getting that ass" if he had to. He'd had a hard life growing up in L.A. He grew up on the streets, raised by a mother with addictive and abusive behaviors. She was a good person but her own issues got in the way. I remember looking at Leo and wanting someone just like him. I was still very needy and wanted to find someone to share my life with, but my own issues kept getting in the way. I realized that my attraction to Leo was putting me in a bad situation. I decided to keep my distance from Paula. I saw that she was unstable and did not want to be caught up in her drama.

I did not succeed very well, as Leo started to come and see me. He was very attracted to me and could not keep his hands off of me. I knew I was doing wrong, but I did not want to stop him. We went out to a movie in Oakland and saw each other a few more times. I told him that I was not comfortable creeping around on the side and not long after he left Paula and moved in with me. It only lasted two weeks. Paula barged into my home and my bedroom and told Leo to get out of bed and come back home. She spoke to him like he was a bad little boy and it was time for him to straighten up. He got dressed and went outside to talk to her and then he got his stuff and went back with her.

I was really hurt but not surprised. I made my choices and this was the outcome I had to accept. After this Paula started to come to my house at night, park on the other side of the street and just sit in her car staring at my house. Several times I just sat at my bedroom window staring back at her. I could see her puffing on her cigarettes, thinking about hurting me – crazy bitch. When I stared back she would drive off after five minutes. I guess it pissed her off that I would stare back. I learned later that Leo was doing hard drugs and I decided I wanted nothing more to do with him. I would not have drugs in my home or around my children.

Aaron opens his school

Aaron started to have problems with Jerrod. More and more students were going to Aaron's classes rather than Jerrod's. It was obvious that everyone enjoyed his teaching and Jerrod felt threatened. When Aaron was discharged from the Air Force in 1992, he moved to Red Bluff where his wife Annie was still stationed, and opened his own martial arts school. I went to and participated in his grand-opening demonstration. Lawrence, the instructor from Fairfax was also there to support the grand opening. I was known for my strength and I enjoyed breaking bricks. Aaron got me a brick to break, but warned me that it was wet and to be careful not to hurt myself. I just smiled and smashed that brick. Lawrence gave me a standing ovation, which made me feel really good and lifted my self-esteem. I went to Red Bluff whenever I could to train under Aaron.

I felt really good about myself. I had a decent job doing medical billing, was making friends, and doing well in martial arts. Despite my poor choices with Leo I was learning how to manage my life. I was gaining better boundaries and starting to find success. After the crap with Paula and with Jerrod snubbing me in the school, I realized it was time to make changes in my life. I wanted to live in a country setting for Tory and Mark and also continue my martial arts training. I decided I needed to move to Red Bluff.

In 1993 I was promoted to 1st degree blackbelt, not because Jerrod wanted to promote me but because everyone was questioning why he still did not He did not want to expose his true resentment towards me. I knew after I was promoted that I would move to Red Bluff and train under Aaron. I had to make plans where to live, how to arrange Tory's care while I worked, and gas money for the commute to work.

Communication with my mother

Around this time I really wanted to call my mom and speak my mind to her. I talked to Sarah about this and felt that I had my own power and was ready to speak to her. I had found an account with my mom's name and personal information through my job. I took her phone number and considered for a couple of weeks. I was getting ready to move and saw this as an opportunity to close doors and start fresh. I wanted to have my say and I could feel the anger towards her, worse now with the knowledge of what she did to me and my kids (what she took from me but could not hang onto because I was stronger than her).

I had a thousand things to tell her and finally called. She answered the phone and I did not say anything at all. I heard her voice and did not want to say anything! I just listened to her. She seemed to know it was me. All she said was "Just speak to me... Say something to me." I felt it was important not to give her any information. If I did she would know how to manipulate me. She just kept saying "Talk to me!" She never asked if I was OK, if my kids were OK, or if we needed anything. After a couple of minutes of prompting me she hung up. I had everything in the world to say to her, but when I called there was nothing to say. It dawned on me that she only wanted to see what space I was in so that she could manipulate me and gain control again. She had no concern for me or my kids. No love at all. I decided to write her the following letter:

To the Mother that ruined my life.
I speak about the horrors you and Dad did to me. You do not want me to talk about it and you do not want me to validate my brothers and sister of your abusive actions to all of us. I got news for you, I do talk about it and I will not stop. You and dad are one of the most heinous parents and I will have nothing to do with you ever. I know what you did to my kids and I will protect them from you and you will never hurt them again.
You will never be a part of my life and you do not represent who I am.
I have claimed my life and it is nothing of what you represent.
No longer your daughter

She responded with a torn piece of paper typed; "I disagree." The address was typed and impersonal. That was the last time I ever corresponded with her.

Moving to Red Bluff

I became friends with a colleague at work, Karen, who was originally from England and had draft horses. She lived on a small ranch near Red Bluff and offered to rent me a trailer on her property. I accepted and moved all my stuff into storage in Red Bluff. Tory and I treated it as camping and a fun adventure. I was able to arrange babysitting in Red Bluff and get organized.

I went to see Aaron to discuss my continued training. I told him I had followed the proper etiquette to have him be my instructor and only asked him to promise one thing: "Promise that you will not make any passes at me or I will kick your ass." I was here to continue my martial arts training, not to be "his girl on the side." I wanted nothing to do with any situation like that any more. He promised me that he would not and did not want me to kick his ass. I still giggle when I think about it. I always shoot from the hip. So I made new friends in Red Bluff and really loved being in the country.

After two months Karen's husband, a red neck asshole, decided he wanted to go hunting and use the trailer I was staying in. He refused my rent money for the month and told Karen that I was harassing him. She tried to make problems at work. I said nothing to her when she confronted me publicly at work, but finally told her that her husband had refused my money and wanted me out. She did not believe me. I told Aaron about the situation and he asked an older couple in the school to help. They enjoyed doing martial arts and their adult son Steven also trained at the school. Tom and Carol took me and Tory into their home. We stayed for about two months until I found a place of my own on ten acres. I felt like I had made a new family with Tom and Carol. They enjoyed my children and called me their daughter. We did family things together and I helped Carol with cleaning the house. I really appreciated their help and support.

Leo makes life changes

Leo was still trying to keep in touch, but I kept turning him away. I knew he was doing drugs and not right with his life. Tom did not like black people and was prejudiced towards Leo. I told them not to worry, that I knew how to handle my business. I had not heard from Leo in seven months. For about two weeks, I kept feeling that death was around him and started to look in the obituaries to see if he had died. Shortly after, I was outside the office on break and saw Leo walking towards me. I could see that he had been beaten up. The whites of his eyes were bloody red. I was shocked to see the condition he was in. I sat down with him and asked what happened. He told me that Paula and two of her sons had attacked him. Paula had taken a baseball bat to his head and the other two had beaten him. He was sent to the hospital ICU for two weeks and had almost died.

I was shocked, realizing the feelings I'd kept having were at the same time he was in the hospital! I took his hand and softly told him that "love" does not do this to people. When you love someone you do not try to kill them. I then asked him "When are you going to respect yourself enough to no longer allow anyone to treat you like this?" My words hit home with him and he realized that Paula had never loved him.

He decided to make changes in his life. He moved out of Paula's house and got a cheap apartment. Unfortunately, this was a drug running place and he was still doing drugs. He crashed his work truck and was fired. I told him that drugs were not the answer and if he was serious about changing his life that meant the drugs needed to stop. It was his choice and he needed to get his life straightened out. I was learning lessons about real friends and needy friends.

Tom could not tolerate Leo and told Carol that I could no longer come around, so one weekend Carol said she would drive Mark back to his residential home after his weekend visit. I came along with Tory and on the way home she began to attack me verbally. I was shocked at her words. She told me that I was in the way, that my life was not right, and Tom did not like what I was doing. She told me that they felt "they were being used." I was really hurt and embarrassed that she told me off like a child in front of my daughter. I had always been honest with them and told her thank you, but I cannot do what you think I should do. As a result we stopped being friends. Again I found conditional love and was tossed aside when I no longer 'cooperated'.

I also learned from Carol that Annie had told her about my family issues. I had confided in Annie and thought she was a friend. I realized that she had told everyone in the school about my issues and I felt very violated and hurt. I began to realize that my friendship with her was one-sided. After talking to Sarah I realized that I was the one who made the phone calls, who initiated and kept the friendship going. I decided to stop calling after learning how she dishonored my confidence. She never called or asked how I was doing. Another lesson learned in life. Fair weather friendships are usually one-sided.

I realized that I had some other friends through Karen who only talked to me when I called. They did not invite me to the horse shows or to do other horse stuff with them. I began to feel that I had no real friends in my life. I went to Aaron about the situation with Annie and wanted to know what he felt about me. He told me that he could not see any of the problems with me that Annie talked about. He could not see that I was different so he had decided to be my friend and ignore what she said. I thanked him for his honesty and also asked about Tom and Carol. He told me that they tended to reject people who did not do what they thought was right. I was still hurt but felt a little better knowing that it wasn't personal.

Making friends

I had made friends in the school, and my two favorites were Randy and Vince. They were also 1st degree blackbelts and I enjoyed training with them. I learned a lot about better boundaries by watching Randy interact with other people. He was a very tall man and kept to himself. He was not very demonstrative but always took time to train with me and help me. He had a good family and wonderful daughters. As I was going through another level of learning life's lessons, I watched Randy to see how he talked and interacted with people, what he said and did not say. I still needed to improve how I interacted with people. I chose to watch Randy because he seemed to be liked by all. I would pay close attention to how he responded to me and if I put him off by what I said or did. I learned a lot by watching him. He never knew how much he taught me. We are still the best of friends and have watched our kids grow up together. He is my martial arts brother.

Vince was the golden boy of the school. He did forms and techniques really well and was very talented. I used to tease him because he was shorter than me, saying he could do better forms because he was closer to the ground. He took my teasing well for the most part. Randy, Vince and I trained together and always made sure we stayed in shape so as not to let the others down and not let anyone get the better of the others. We were competitive, but in a good way. Like siblings, we always did things together with some bickering, but if anyone came into our circle and disrupted us we had each others backs.

Sarah told me that this was a great situation because I was interacting with positive people and could learn and grow in my interpersonal skills. I worked very hard to understand appropriate boundaries. I was able to get past the harder things in my recovery and focus on refining myself and the damage I was still carrying. Even if it hurt my ego I forced myself to see my mistakes (how I said things, if I was speaking to loudly or with too much force). I spent this time looking at my faults and strengths – how I interacted with people and how they reacted or acted towards me. I knew I had a strong personality and I needed to learn how to find a balance. I spent a long time refining my interpersonal skills and taking an honest look at myself, how I reacted and why. I slowly gained confidence in my skills, refining them and learning positive ways of correcting my mistakes. I also began to define who I was. I learned through experience about needy people, toxic people, healthy people and everyone in between.

Chapter 6. Questioning my life

Despite all this learning, I still felt deep inside like I was the "damaged goods" no one wanted to be around. The different person with the "extreme abuse issues" who did not fit in. I have been working on better decisions and better boundaries, but I began to see that I was still on the "outside." I was accepted in my martial arts school but that was all. When class was over I went home and I was alone. I had no personal success in finding someone to share my life with. I didn't think it was a situation of feeling sorry for myself. It was the reality of seeing the difference between my life and other people and their lives. They had family, friends, and extended family. They "belonged" in life. I was realizing the huge difference between my life experiences and those of most people. Facing the reality that you had parents who abused you and that you were never allowed to live your life was a hard concept to work through.

At the same time I was starting to get angry with my higher power. I still felt a pull towards native and pagan beliefs. I started to go to moon circle with other women, but I still had a hard time inside. I could see so many people who knew nothing about the way I was abused and raised. That gap was really hard to deal with. I could no longer see a reason why I should live my life. I began to feel the full force of the sorrow about what happened to me. I could not feel inside a reason to live. My soul felt empty and there were not enough rewards in my life to fill the empty hole. My feelings at the time were why go through all this healing and recovery work only to be alone and on the outside. How could I create a relationship with anybody when I had all these extreme abuse issues? Why would anyone want to be with me?

This was a very serious time in my life. I started to get really angry at the "Mormon Jesus" again. I remembered being around four or five years old, going to church and being taught how Jesus loved everybody including me. I thought maybe my Sunday school teacher was right and Jesus did love me. I remember before I went to bed I would pray very hard, asking Jesus to please love me enough to take me back to heaven because I could not live another day in that house. I told Jesus it was more than I could bear. In my prayers I begged for Jesus to love me enough to take me back to him so I would no longer have to face another day of horror. Every night I prayed and believed that when I went to sleep I would wake up in heaven. Every night before I went to bed I said that prayer asking Jesus to love me enough to take me to heaven. Everyday I opened my eyes and was still in that house facing another day of horror.

One night my father heard me praying to Jesus to take me back to heaven. The next night my father and mother made me pray to Jesus in front of other members. They told me to pray to Jesus and ask him to come down and stop them from hurting me. He made me pray to Jesus while they hit me, spit on me, and kicked me, forcing me to ask Jesus to make them stop. I prayed and prayed and Jesus never came to stop them. They kept ridiculing me and my prayers and forcing me to perform sex acts on them. My mother got a couple of kittens and made me pray to Jesus to stop her from hurting them. I prayed with all my heart for Jesus to stop my mother and Jesus never came. The kittens were killed and my father stood there and told me that Jesus did not love me. He told me that not only did Jesus not love me, that I was not worth his time. When a child goes through something like that, the reality of not seeing Jesus come to help you is a very clear picture that you are not worth shit. I could see myself then and all the feelings I went through.

I became really angry at the Mormon Jesus because he did not come to help that little girl nor did he take her back to heaven. Once again I was in a state of "to hell with that Mormon Jesus" and any other higher power that may exist. If he did not want me then he could not have me now. If the Mormon Jesus could not take time for a little girl, and prevent her from being horrifically abused in his church, then I would not have anything to do with him! No matter how my anger at the Mormon Jesus made me want to deny any higher power I could not in my heart deny that there was a higher power. Deep in my heart I knew that there was a higher power and that this higher power did not represent the actions of my parents or the Mormon Jesus. I knew I needed to redefine what a higher power was. I knew it was not the Mormon Jesus or anything to do with the Mormon Church. I guess saying "the Mormon Jesus" gave me permission to be angry at the higher power that I had prayed to and not been saved by when I was little.

I had every right to be angry and needed to vent this huge mass of anger towards this higher power that did not help me. This anger raged in me for many years and as a result I began to lose my inner fire to live. I could see such a difference among the vast majority of people not subjected to such atrocities. Remembering the heinous actions of my parents and church members made it very hard to have any clarity of purpose. I worked very hard to free myself from my perpetrators only to find myself "different," an outsider with no place to belong in life. Why should I go through all this healing of horrific abuses only to find myself still "different"? This took a hard toll on me. I could not get past the anger and grief. Why was I the one that had to endure all these horrors and recovery only to be left with no one? I found myself yelling at my higher power. I would just vent all my anger, knowing inside that it was OK to do this. It was like a little child yelling at his parents without understanding the bigger picture. I felt that I had a right to my anger, but I also realized that my inner spark was dying. My soul needed to feel a reason to live. It had to come from inside not outside. I began to pray for a reason to live. I needed to feel a spark of life. This was a very dark time for me. The pain was very strong and I could not see a way through it.

I decided to end my life. If I ended my life I could not let my kids go back to my family and the cult, so I would take Tory's and Mark's lives with mine. I started to plan how I would do this. I could no longer face being on the outside, never belonging anywhere or connected to anyone. To live through a life of atrocities only to be damaged goods. I reconciled myself that if the Mormon Jesus was true and I was going to hell after suicide, I planned on fighting. Even though I did not see a reason to live, I still had that raging anger inside of me. I still thought "What if the Mormon Jesus would be waiting for me?" I knew in my heart that what the Mormon Jesus allowed to happen to kids was wrong. I could not stand idle and I would fight him every step of the way into Hell. Despite my overwhelming grief, my strong will to fight back still raged inside of me.

Leo comes back

The day before I was going to kill us I heard someone walking up my porch steps. I looked out the door and it was Leo. I had sent him away months ago, but he had followed me from my work. He looked like a rejected puppy trying to say he was sorry. I could not believe my eyes. The man I really loved and wanted was on my porch. He apologized to me and told me that he wanted to be with me. He had walked away from everything and everybody in Chico and wanted only me. I felt a small spark in my soul and decided to let him back into my life and decided to keep living. Leo was the one who began to heal my heart and the wounds of my soul. He gave me a reason to live and the pain slowly began to go away, but the spark in my soul was still an issue.

It was December 1994 and my landlord found out that Leo was living with me. She was an old lady and from the school that "whites" and "blacks" do not live together. The plumbing in the mobile home broke, creating a large hole in the floor. She gave me an eviction notice when I told her about the plumbing damage and I had to leave just before Christmas. I could not believe that she did that to me, but I was lucky and found a small two-bedroom house in Red Bluff and moved into town. Mark's residential center give me presents for Tory and Mark and food. I was really hurt that I could not have a Christmas for my kids.

In February, Paula decided to go down every street in Red Bluff to find where we lived. We were shocked that she found us, but I would not answer the door and called the police. The police came and told her to leave, giving her a ticket for parking the wrong way on a one-way street. She came again the following month with her minister. I refused to answer the door, wanting nothing to do with either of them. Silence was the best way to keep the garbage out. The minister walked around my house knocking on all my windows to get my attention, which I thought that was very poor behavior on his part. I finally told him through the door that Leo and I were not interested in talking to him and especially not to Paula. I explained to him that their marriage was over and the divorce was already filed. He understood and left. Paula came over and started banging on my door. I called the police again and she finally left.

Drugs

In June I realized that Leo went to Chico for drugs. That same day, Paula came again to cause problems. I finally went out the door and she was across the street yelling at me. I could tell she was high as a kite. When she shut up I told her that her marriage was over. It was me that Leo came home to not her. I informed her that she needed to face this fact and that she may be the reason why her marriage did not work. I pointed out that I was nowhere in the picture when she jumped Leo with her two sons and the baseball bat, which may have been the determining factor in the failure of her fourth marriage. She was stunned that I spoke such truth to her. I told her that if she wanted a piece of me to come on over and see what she got. Why come all this way for nothing? She would not come over and I yelled that if she was so tough and wanted me so bad now was her chance. She refused and I knew that unless she had someone to back her up she was too much of a coward to fight on her own. I looked at her and told her she was nothing but ghetto trash. I went back into the house and called the police again. That was the last time she came up to harass us. We had a restraining order put on her, but she would no longer come up. I decided not to update the order once it expired. I felt that I had made my point and given her a chance to get her hands on me that she passed up. If she was going to be stupid again I would have grounds for a permanent restraining order. After Paula left I was so upset. I felt I was being played and packed all of Leo's personal belongings and put it in the back of his truck.

When he came home I told him that we needed to take a walk.

I did not want Tory to see or hear what I had to say. As we walked I explained to him that I would not have drugs in my home or around my kids. It was not an option I would tolerate. If his drug dealer could take better care of him and give him a better piece of ass than I could, his bags were in the back of his truck and he could move in with the dealer tonight, since this drug dealer was so damn important to him. I made it very clear that if he decided to go then, there would be no co-dependent bullshit of "OK, I forgive you and will give you another chance."

Either he could stay with me and off drugs or he could walk out my door right now and use all the drugs he wants. I gave him my word that if he walked out that night I would never speak to him again. It would be over with no option of coming back. Since drugs were more important than me then he could have his drugs and end this right now. If he tried to come back I would ignore him or call the police. It really shook him up and he knew I meant every word. Leo promised me that he would never do that to me again and wanted to stay. I told him that I was not responsible for his actions only my own. If he messed up again, I would take the responsibility of kicking him out and I better never see that bullshit again. Not long afterwards Leo went back into the union and I've never known him to touch drugs again.

CHAPTER 7. WORK AND THE EMPOWERED DYSFUNCTIONAL

My mother taught me how to do medical billing. After working in several jobs in this field I noticed certain themes. People have different perceptions about toxic and healthy, but they always bring their garbage to the workplace. People make decisions based on their own issues, and punish those who are different. I learned a lot about myself and saw the same things in every work place. Someone always had a problem with a strong, intelligent woman. I had to strengthen my interpersonal skills to deal with these empowered toxic people and I hated it. I had to examine my propensity to shoot from the hip and grab the bull by the horns, toss it to the ground and make it say "uncle." I had to see my faults and make changes where necessary.

I always found that I could only tolerate a certain amount of garbage before I started to toss it back. If I were bothered, I would always bring issues to the attention of my colleagues and supervisors. It always amazed me that they never realized if they had just left me alone they would not have had a problem. I will not own other peoples garbage. I did learned to keep my mouth shut and speak in more refined ways, but I still hate working in medical billing. I guess I am far too independent, strong-willed, and intelligent to be confined to a work space and dysfunctional, micro-managed, toxic environment. Corporate America sucks!

By 1996, I decided to find a job closer to home. I was tired of commuting to Chico and realized I no longer needed any therapy. I had gained many skills to cope with my life. I was getting better boundaries and was able to manage my life. Tory was older and Sarah felt she no longer needed therapy. Sarah supported my decision to end therapy and told me that if I were not feeling secure I would not have moved out of Chico. She told me that she would always be there if I ever needed her help. I can not thank Sarah enough for taking me in and walking with me through all the heinous garbage I had to recover from. I know she never got much money from Victim Witness but she stood by me all the same. There are never enough words and appreciation to repay her for what she has done for me and my kids. Some things can never be repaid.

Leo was working 6-7 months of the year and was off in winter. It was hard to survive the winters with a cut in pay as he did not have a permanent job and the union sent him to temporary jobs. Many times I wanted him to leave the union and get a different job, but Leo would not leave the union. He enjoyed working on heavy equipment and wanted to keep doing what he loved. The years he was an apprentice and promoting to Journeyman were hard years. I started working in a medical group and it was OK. They were very disorganized with poor billing information and I spent more time writing off things that could have been paid than what should truly have been written off. Being of strong mind I could no longer stay there. I wanted to fix the problem, but the powers that be had no inclination to improve the existing set up. I find it amazing that empowered dysfunctional management continues to be the norm. When you propose simple solutions their issues get in the way.

In 1996 I became the office manager for an East Indian doctor. It only lasted a few months as I soon saw that he was very cheap and had "legal entanglements." He also had very inappropriate behaviors with his back office nurse. He would measure the width of her bottom in front of his patients, make comments about how fat she looked, and laughed about it. The nurse idolized him and saw no wrong in it. I realized she did not have appropriate boundaries and did not see how poorly she was being treated. The doctor did not want me talking to her and "giving her ideas." He could see that I did not put up with that sort of crap. He once tried to pinch my ribs. I looked at him and said "I will only say it one time, do not do that. If it happens again I will discuss it in a manner that will not be misunderstood." He was not stupid.

He tried to get me to commit billing fraud and each time I pointed out that it was fraud and I had no intention of going to jail for him. His wife worked as a private dentist in the adjacent office. The state police raided her practice and she was investigated for dental fraud. I could not believe the crap these two got themselves into and knew it was time to get out another job. He finally updated his computer system and paid for a new billing program. I did the conversion to electronic billing and told him that claims would take longer for awhile due to the conversion. For two weeks I was only able to send paper claims and everyday he came in and ask where his money was. After a week of this daily questioning I asked "Why do you ask me the same thing everyday? The answer is still the same!" He got angry and raised his hand to strike me. I told him "I can do that, we can walk outside right now and take care of this but your ass will not be coming in the same way it went out! !" He was so angry that his chin started quivering and he finally walked away.

I had been offered another job near Chico in Long-Term Care billing. A couple of days later the doctor came and asked again where his money was and I gave the same answer "Why are you asking me this?" He raised his hand again and said he was a boxing champion. I told him that was nice but I would mess him up for life so he could take his best shot. He walked away and I picked up all my belongings and walked out never to return. I knew Leo would be upset and want to "discuss this" with him. He would not tolerate anyone treating me like this and would have hurt him. I did not want Leo going to jail for this idiot so I left.

Prior to my leaving this employment, I had made friends with the back office nurse who told me about a house she had for sale. She knew I wanted to buy a home and told me that I could qualify to take over the mortgage. Leo and I went to see the house and decided to move to Marysville. After we moved in and began paying rent I began the process of qualifying for the mortgage. I qualified with no problems but learned there were back taxes that needed to be paid. She had lied to me about the whole deal. I was really angry, as I had moved to this home to purchase it and she refused to pay her back taxes. I could not take over the mortgage until this was paid and I realized that she hoped I would bail her out of what she owed. I had no intention of doing so. I missed living in Red Bluff and decided to find a home to buy there. Tory was attending Junior High-school in Red Bluff and wanted to stay there. In March 1997 I bought a house in Red Bluff and we moved back.

98

Long-term care billing

I started doing long-term care billing and looked forward to learning something new. It did not take long to become proficient. There were about ten different billing/accounting clerks. We were given three to four different facilities and did all billing, trust funds, levels of care for each day billed, maintained a census, and when patients went to hospital. Instead of being in cubicles we all had separate rooms. No one could see or talk to each other unless they went to another office. The rooms were small with a big window next to the door. If management walked by they could see if you were working or not. It was a very detail-oriented job and I was able to improve efficiency for each facility and keep all billing current.

I began to see that our manager and lead staff were very passive-aggressive. The owner of the company and the manager were very close and this is where I learned about nepotism. The manager was a very cold woman. She supported her favorite employees and anyone else could do nothing right. I would walk past the offices of employees she did not like and see them crying because of her. It was very unhealthy and there was no reprieve. It was not long before she started on me, telling me that I was not doing a good job because I had money on the books that was 60 to 90 days old. I had very little money at 60 to 90 days and nothing at 120 days, and noticed that her pet employees had much worse records and were not reprimanded. I pointed this out to her but of course it did me no favors.

By October of 1998 I'd had enough. I just lost it. I began to panic that she was closing in on me and would destroy my life and I could do nothing about it. I told my doctor about my anxieties and she put me on stress leave and counseling for a month. I'd had enough of walking into jobs and finding that I was forced to be the victim of office garbage. No matter how hard I tried to work things out in a positive way I was always treated badly. I never returned to that job and decided to try a temp agency. If I did not like somewhere I could go to another job.

Temping

In November 1998 I started work with a medical billing company through the temp agency. Again I saw the same dysfunctional crap. One woman there could not deal with a strong woman and went out of her way to make my life miserable. She had a nervous disposition and was never still, working very fast to keep herself very busy. I realized that the accounts they maintained made it harder to collect money, but any suggestion I made was received with rude comments. They made their money by sending out volume rather than quality of claims. Since staff got paid for each claim it was to their benefit to keep things unpaid. I ignored her from then on and concentrated on doing quality work. She did not like that either and felt the need to control me. She soon found out that I was not a person you could control or threaten, which only exacerbated the situation. Fortunately, one of the hospital accounts I was working on was noticed by the hospital billing staff. They were impressed with how the money came in when I took over this account and became interested in me working for them.

Cardiology

After several months with the first temp job I told the agency I did not want to work there anymore. They sent me to a Cardiology office in Chico. I enjoyed working there and the office was nice. I really enjoyed the drug representatives coming in with free food for lunch. It was good food too. The tone of the office was quiet and polite. Given my strong personality, it was hard and at times I was blind to my own behavior. Even though I did a great job and the money flowed in, it was clear I did not fit in. The lead biller became a friend and I was accepted by the other workers, but the supervisor was stuck in her antiquated management style. If your behavior did not fit with her value system then you were of no worth. Because I brought in lots of money and cleaned up their accounts I was tolerated. I stayed until May 1999.

Hospital billing

The hospital that I'd done billing for through the temp agency found me and made me an offer to work for them in Chico. I was really flattered that they wanted me and interviewed with the supervisor and the lead Medi-cal Biller. It was new for me and I decided to work for the hospital billing office. I also worked part-time at the cardiologist office until my replacement was trained and able to take over.

I thought I would have a better job and be working with better people, but I soon found the same problems. My boss was a manipulative person and the lead Medi-cal person, Lyn, was hated by everyone in the office. She was a bit crazy, and would focus on a person and give them a hard time. Again I found myself working in a place with people who had their issues. No matter how many problem solving skills I had there was always someone who could not stand me. Lyn was my nemesis. She had recruited me then turned around and started harassing me.

Again I found myself in a situation where women had their issues, and when a bunch of women get together, drama occurs. Whenever it focused on me, I relied on what I learned in recovery to manage my life, and applied it in the workplace. I worked there for 4 years and despite the continued efforts to harass me, when I did leave, it was on my own terms.

Jerrod's fall

I learned that Jerrod had been arrested for sexually assaulting a teenager. The Chico DA called to question me about my interactions with Jerrod. They wanted me to be a witness for the prosecution. I had no problem in standing up and speaking the truth about Jerrod. If he was guilty of sexual assault then he needed to be prosecuted. Angela was in complete denial, which surprised me since she had seen that he always had women in his office with the door closed or in their home. Jerrod knew to hide anything to do with molesting

101

children/teens from me. I knew the victim, who was a foster child with one of the families in his school. The police got Jerrod on tape talking to her in a sexually suggestive way on the phone. They arrested him on several counts of child molestation and wanted to prosecute him. In the end he did a deal with the DA, and agreed to plead guilty for jail time instead of prison. He was registered as a child sex offender and could no longer teach anyone under the age of 18.

The Grandmaster asked about the final outcome of the trial and when he learned that he had to serve time and be a registered sex offender, Jerrod was stripped of his rank and kicked out of our martial arts organization. Angela tried to continue the school for a time but it soon closed. Jerrod lost everything. His career was over.

2nd degree promotions

By 1996 Randy, Vince and I were testing for our 2nd degree blackbelts. Aaron was very hard on us in testing, but none of us ever gave up. When you reach 1st degree blackbelt you have just graduated from kindergarten. There are more techniques, weapons and forms to learn. You are not considered a master until you are promoted to 5th degree. I had been training for six years and I made many friends. The Grandmaster and his family knew me and respected me. I was sticking with it.

I noticed for some time that Aaron would teach Vince and Randy techniques before I would be taught. If I missed a blackbelt class, Randy and Vince would be taught new techniques and the following week I would not. Aaron just told me that I did not train enough. I disagreed but it was to deaf ears. Randy always trained with me and we supported each other. I mentioned this to Randy and he would remind Aaron that I had not been taught. Usually Aaron would teach me when Randy brought it to his attention. Sometimes Randy would teach me to keep me caught up and he always stood by me. I came to realize that Aaron had his issues with women in martial arts. Aaron was a funny man. Unless you were a guy he could not relate to you. I once heard him say that women could not teach men martial arts. He is a good man but had an underlining nervousness that always reminded me of a pressure cooker with steam escaping. He meant well, but had his shortcomings like anybody else. I accepted him for who he was and kept training.

By this time Aaron separated from his wife and started divorce proceedings. He moved to a town near Auburn and opened another school. He was running two schools and blackbelt testing was now held in his new school. Our Grandmaster had moved to Texas to be more centrally located. His oldest son, SJ, stayed in San Francisco and ran the school there. Randy and Vince got promoted to 2nd degree blackbelt but I was not promoted because I had missed a test due to illness and not been allowed to make it up. I was really hurt, because I felt I trained as much as Randy and Vince and had seen other blackbelts make up tests. Aaron began to be more critical of me, but after the next testing I was finally promoted to 2nd degree blackbelt.

When I was promoted to 2nd Degree, Senior Master and SJ came from San Francisco, and I shook Senior Master's hand to thank him for coming. Kay had also come along with other teachers and students. I had seen Kay in different activities over the years. Ever since the incident with John, Kay was either nice or she would snub me. I never knew how she would behave and was really irritated by her. I let her actions get the best of me for a long time. When I turned to Kay at promotion to shake her hand she turned her back on me in front of Senior Master. I was really embarrassed and angry . Once again I see Kay snubbing me for unknown reasons. That was the last straw. I was so angry I went into Aaron's office to take a time out. Aaron came in and asked me what was wrong and I explained to him what Kay had done. I told him I wanted to go out and ring her neck, but etiquette was the most important thing in our martial arts. I did not want to disgrace myself or Aaron but I'd had enough of her behavior. He told me that the best thing to do was to do and say nothing, to just ignore her and keep my distance. I agreed and from that day I ignored her. I did not speak to her for many years.

After promotion I continued to train under Aaron. I really loved doing martial arts and my skills continued to improve. I still could

103

not do very graceful forms, but I was confident in techniques and self defense sets. I was still very strong in sparring but had worked hard to develop control. Most of the men were careful when sparring me.

I still had more to learn. For example, one day I was paired for line sparring with Sam, a fairly new student who was my height, 5'6," and weighed about 140lbs. He was a nice man but seemed to have a napoleon complex. He came on really strong and was hitting hard. I stopped and told him that he was hitting too hard and needed to calm down. We started again, he continued hitting aggressively, and I stopped again and told him to tone it down. Sam came in hitting even harder. I looked at him and began to feel upset. I proceeded to take my sparring up a few notches and backed him up against the wall to show him he did not have the skills to take me on. He was up against the wall while I fed him lefts and rights with no break. Randy saw this, stopped the sparring and scolded me. Aaron had seen me ask Sam to use better control and spoke up on my behalf. Sam was no worse for it and used better control with me from then on. However, after class Randy took me into the office and told me off. He told me that I was a blackbelt and had a responsibility to set a better example. I was expected to act at a higher level. I thought about it and knew he was right. I should have stopped sparring and let Randy or Aaron deal with Sam.

I learned a lesson about the responsibilities of my rank and that I needed to present myself with more self control and observe a higher standard. I needed to make better decisions about my own actions while training. The martial art I studied emphasized martial traditions that are thousands of years old. We were expected to understand this traditional code of honor and integrity and live our lives as martial artists. Master SJ says it best "It is not the destination, it is the journey." Of course he also says "We need more practice!" I was learning what a real martial artist is, and about a life of honor and integrity not just a rank. I wanted this way of life. I realized through martial arts I was creating a path of healing for myself without the help of a therapist.

Tory's horses

When I first moved to Red Bluff and lived on ten acres, a friend gave me an Arab horse, Silly. Though I don't really like Arabs, this was a horse for Tory. I wanted Tory to have the same experiences as I'd had with horses. When we moved, Silly went to stay on Mary's ranch. I met Mary through Carol, though Carol lost her friendship because she interfered in the personal life of Mary's son. Mary is a strong woman of Scottish lineage and a true horsewoman. Her knowledge of horses is vast, while as a talented musician she can play Chopin with the best of them. She can draw and paint beautifully. When I first went to her ranch she showed me all of her horses in her barn. I fell in love with her horses and knew they came from God's Stable. She had well-bred quality horses and I dreamed of affording one just like hers. I worked with Tory in teaching dressage with Silly. I would ride him from time to time but Tory was the one who rode him the most. Eventually I had to sell Silly because I could not afford him and he was not working out for Tory.

When Mary found a retired cutting horse, Doc, that a friend gave to her. She asked if I could afford the board if she gave him to Tory. I said yes and we planned to surprise Tory. Doc was 21 years old, a retired cutting horse with great conformation except for a sway back. As long as the saddle was on he was a great looking quarter horse. I called Leo and he told Tory that Mary needed her help gathering up some cows that had gotten loose. I had Doc saddled up and waiting in the arena for her. Tory had taken lessons on Mary's horse Biddy and was expecting to ride her again. Tory got to the ranch Mary told Tory to go to the arena and get her horse. Tory walked to the arena and saw Doc. She stood there wondering why Biddy was not saddled up. Mary told her that Doc was her horse. Tory was shocked and could not believe that she had a horse. I told her that he was a great horse and retired from cutting. She quickly fell in love with Doc. He was perfect for her and he tolerated her like any old man with kids, with lots of sighs and groans. She took lessons from Mary and sometimes from Doug, a renowned trainer. Mary always

105

helped Doug turn back cows while he trained horses. Tory wanted to do High-school Rodeo and cutting. When Tory turned 18, I took a picture of her with Doc like the picture I had of me at that age with my horse Bob. I put Tory's picture next to mine and told her that when her daughter grows up we will get a picture of her when she is 18 with her horse. I was establishing a family tradition.

My martial arts brother dies

James, Tom and Carol's son, had been diagnosed three years earlier (at the age of 29) with Lou Gerrig's disease. I really cared about James and looked to him as my brother. He was fun and I loved training with him. I saw that James had lost the majority of his muscle movement and it was very sad for me to see him like that. He had to sit in a chair and could do nothing. His wife Helen was taking full care of him while also being expected to clean Tom and Carol's house. I was angry that Carol made her clean her house while she was taking care of Carol's son and grandsons, but in Tom and Carol's mind they were helping to pay the bills so she needed to clean their house. Helen always accommodated them and never complained. It was hard for me to watch her run herself ragged and keep my mouth shut.

James loved the Pittsburg Steelers and I wrote to the Steelers about James and how he loved "the Bus." They sent back a signed picture of "the Bus" that I gave to James. He loved it and even though he could not talk I the greatfulness in his eyes. James loved that I always shot from the hip. I told him about the doctor who tried to slap me and telling him "We can do that but you will not walk back in the same way you went out." He loved my story and laughed and laughed. He then told me through Helen that he was sorry about the way his parents treated me. He said that they cut people off when they don't do what they think is right. I told him thank you and not to worry.

I checked on James from time to time and he appreciated that I kept contact. He seemed to take me under his wing as his little sis-

106

ter and even taught me to change brake pads. At Aaron's daughter's wedding reception, James took me and Leo aside and told us not to have kids. He explained that having a mixed child would be hard on that child. Leo and I just smiled knowing he was saying it out of love and told him we had no intention of having kids. The things you remember.

When James died I lost my martial arts brother. His funeral was at a Christian church in town. I had a hard time walking into that church but I did for James, and sat with Leo and other blackbelts from the school. I still miss him. I visited Helen and the boys sometimes. Helen and I would always catch up with each other and our children's' lives. Tom and Carol eventually moved to Texas. Not long after James died they began snubbing Helen. They would visit the boys but treat Helen as if she was no longer family. Helen moved on in her life and her boys are grown up. The eldest looks just like his dad.

Chapter 8. My own school

In 2001 Tory graduated from High-school. I had decided that when Tory graduated I would open my own martial arts school. I knew I wanted to teach, but my first priority was Tory and being a mother. Now she needed me less and was ready to move on with her life as an adult.

I chose a location in Chico and sent the paperwork and fees to headquarters. I was told they wanted me to speak to the Grandmaster at the next tournament in March. I was not sure why and became very nervous. When the tournament finally came, I spoke to the Grandmaster's wife about the issue. She responded that they needed to talk to me and Kay about my school. I could not believe my ears. What did Kay have to do with this? My proposed school was well beyond the 20 mile minimum distance from her school. I had to bring Kay over, and despite the years in which we hadn't spoken she still managed to be rude. Kay told us that I would be too close to her school. I explained that I would be over 20 miles away and was within the guidelines to be able to have a school. Then she said one of her students had a club close by. I informed them that he was fifteen miles from me. Then she said she planned to open a school near me soon. I looked at Grandmaster's wife and said she would be ten miles away. I offered to get a map and show her. Then Grandmaster's wife started talking to Kay in Korean and shaking her finger at her. After a couple of minutes, Kay scuffed her feet and said in English that she never gets her way, trying to be comical. Grandmaster had joined us when his wife began speaking in Korean. When they were finished, Grandmaster told us to be friends now and no more problems. We agreed and he made us shake hands. I decided to give Kay a hug to kill her with kindness. I thought she would be sick but she held herself well. I began to realize that my experiences from the time I no longer saw Kay until now were learning and healing lessons in life. These situations were not aimed at me personally, but just life and people inter-mixing with each other. I realized I began to see myself no longer as the person who came from extreme issues and different from everyone else, but just as a person inter-acting with other people.

Starting My Own School

I was granted permission to open my school and be an officially licensed instructor. I could not afford my own facility so I started through the Chico Parks department, teaching once a week. I had two students my first month and remember being nervous about where these students came from and how they had heard about me. I was able to teach all the same and realized I had a knack for teaching. It was a nice surprise. I was able to increase to two days and then three days a week. One of these evenings was at a school and at times I would be told at the last minute that they needed the room. It was frustrating, but I managed to make it work and needed to keep teaching to make my school bigger. The first year I averaged eight active students, the second year sixteen. I was still working fulltime in hospital billing, but managed on a flex schedule that was very helpful.

I began teaching in the after-school programs at a junior high-school as a contractor for the county. They assigned me two schools in the ghetto. I did not care about the locations, knowing that if you are right with yourself and who you are then things will be OK. The site coordinator at one school had no interest in organizing the classes. He stuck me in the gym with over 50 students and it was a disaster. I started to teach and of course got the usual pre-teen obnoxious behavior. I ended up sending out all but three students. I was not going to allow them to run over me. The site coordinator did not last long and the next one, a native american man named Stan, was great to work with. He had interested kids fill a sign up sheet for my classes and got me a small room so the other kids could play basketball. I had to relax my instruction and just keep them busy with forms, falling and techniques. If they were good I would let them spar.

One student, Tyrese, was very smart and hyperactive. He would

109

come for my class, run out to play some basketball, and then come back in and do my class again. I told him he was a smart young man, talented in martial arts, and he needed to settle down and start training to see how much he could achieve. His older brother Daunte started classes too. Tyrese was very fast with his hands and I was impressed with his talent. One of Tyrese's teachers called me, wanting to know what I was doing with him. I told her what I taught and she commented that whatever it was to keep it up. She told me he had improved in his classwork and grades. I had not considered that my classes could do something like that.

During one my classes, one of the young black girls informed me that I was white and what could I know about her. I turned around and told her that my mother (my mother-in-law) was black and did she have a problem with that? It really shocked her because she only saw white. I proceeded to tell her that I loved my mother and that half my family was black and did she have a problem with that too? I asked if she wanted to talk to my mother right now. She back peddled and I saw that my words shook her up a bit. She was not ready for a white person to come back so strong. The next week she apologized for what she said. I just smiled and gave her a hug and told her just don't judge a book by its cover. You never know the path a person walks.

What helped me alot is what I had learned long ago in college - that positive reinforcement was the best teacher. I learned about different learning modalities and how to teach each student. It was becoming apparent to me that I had a talent in teaching and I really loved it. I really looked forward to teaching all my students and being an good influence in their lives.

After almost two years, I could no longer teach the after-school program while working fulltime and teaching the adults four nights a week. I needed a break, but I did not want to lose Tyrese and Daunte. I asked their mom if I could pick them up and take them to my school to train. Lorrie lived with a friend and was struggling with SSI disability payments. I really liked her and knew she was doing her best to raise two boys knowing that their Dad died when they

110

were young. She agreed and I kept in contact with her about the boys and their training. We became good friends as I collected the boys two to three times a week for training. Tyrese trained consistently and really excelled. He made friends with everyone in the class and everyone loved him. Daunte eventually quit but would come from time to time.

My school was in better accommodations and I had a steady flow of students in and out of my classes. It was not much but it kept flowing. I was able to use two park facilities four times a week and no longer had to worry about being kicked out of the gym without notice when there was an event. I hated that inconsideration. I started a turtle tots program for kids 3 to 6 years old. I was now teaching martial arts and a pre-martial arts class for little kids.

As the years went by Tyrese kept training. Even when he moved out of town he would come and stay with me. His mother called me his other mother. He worked on Mary's ranch for a summer to earn enough money to pay for his blackbelt testing. He did home schooling, so it was easy for him to stay with me during training and testing. Leo and I came to love Tyrese as family.

After a year of testing, I could see that at age 16 the temptations of drugs and alcohol were hitting him. His brother moved in with his cousin and started drinking and smoking. Daunte started to train in cage fighting, which I do not approve of as it promotes a very negative form of violence. Even though I did not agree with it, I still accepted him. I had spent several years teaching him a better path, but Tyrese finally moved in with his brother. I knew it would not be long before he is doing the same things his brother did. I lost contact with him when he did not show up for testing. It has been almost a year and he never called. I know he needs to walk his path and learn from his mistakes. I have taught him a good way and it is up to him to find that for himself. I hope he will come back one day. Everyone in the school still asks about him and loves him. My school door will always be open.

Aaron marries again

Aaron began dating again and took out several different ladies. I knew they were not quite the right on just by the way he acted around them. I had known him for almost 10 years and still called him my friend and teacher. During our 3rd degree testings at Aaron's school near Auburn, I saw that he was with a very beautiful blond lady named Sara. I could tell by his body language he was head over heels and I knew right then that he would marry her. He introduced me to Sara and as I shook her hand I could feel her spirit. She was a very grounded person and her soul held much wisdom. I really liked her and thought she would be a good grounding person for Aaron. It wasn't long before he proposed to her. They had a wonderful wedding and the reception was at her parent's beautiful property in the foothills. The ceremony was at a small church and blackbelts from the school and instructors from other schools came. We did a sword ceremony and had Sarah walk under our swords up the aisle. It was great to see everyone from the martial arts community in California come to the wedding and celebrate Aaron and Sara's vows. The marriage was a good one and I saw that Aaron was much happier then he had ever been. I was glad that he found someone to share his life with.

3rd degree promotions and falling out with Aaron

In 2002, Aaron decided it was time for Vince, Randy and I to be promoted to 3rd degree blackbelt. Aaron had been promoted to 4th degree and for any instructor to have three students continue training together for over ten years was a special occasion. I was excited to be promoted to 3rd degree. I was passing the half-way mark to becoming a Master and this time I would be promoted with my blackbelt buddies.

I arranged private lessons with Aaron, to begin training for my 4th degree blackbelt, because I could no longer train regularly in the school due to my own teaching obligations. Over the next six months

I scheduled many private lessons, but Aaron always cancelled at the last minute and I only had four lessons in that time frame. I started to wonder what was wrong, but never managed to find a chance to talk with him. I invited Aaron and Sarah, along with some other friends to my school for a promotion demonstration and potluck. Sarah told me she was really impressed with my school and was interested to know why the majority of my students were men. I said it just happened that way. Aaron mentioned the same thing and acted strange about it. I guess in his mind women can't teach men successfully.

At the next tournament several blackbelt ladies were sitting and talking as we always did. Terry, a blackbelt of Aaron's, suggested that all of us should get together to train and support each other. Janet, another of his blackbelts who had just started her school in the foothills, also thought it was a good idea. We talked about how blackbelt women needed to support each other and how fun it would be to train together, and of course it would include going out to lunch and socializing. Terry suggested we train at my school once a month. I liked the idea generally, but was a little uncomfortable with it being done in my school. This conversation attracted other lady blackbelts who also supported the idea. I finally said I would discuss it with Aaron as highest ranking blackbelt in the area. When I called him about it he became really angry, asking how I would like if he took my blackbelts from me. I was shocked that he thought I was trying to steal blackbelts from him. I told that I just wanted to see if he wanted to run it or give me permission to do so, but it was like talking to a wall. He accused me of stealing his blackbelts and having bad etiquette then hung up on me. I was completely devastated and cried for several days. Why were his male blackbelts getting together to train and have fun but something similar with the women was seen as stealing? I could not understand, but when I tried to call again he just hung up.

I felt betrayed, but decided that the only thing that made sense was that he was threatened by me and did not want to teach me at all. I began to realize, that with his recent behavior of always cancelling my private lessons and how he acted at my school demonstration and potluck, that he had no intention of teaching me after my 3rd degree promotion. I began to see that perhaps he was threatened by my success. His extreme reaction made this the only answer that made sense. I did not want to believe it. I had been his student and friend for over ten years. We had watched our children grow up together, had celebrated life's events, and cried together when we lost mutual friends. How could he act like this and not give me the benefit of the doubt?

When Aaron finally talked to me, he said Terry insisted that she had never suggested training and wasn't interested. I responded by saying Terry was obviously back-peddling and I told him Janet would backup my story. In response to his question of my students wanting to train with him, it would be their choice and I would support their decision. I realized that he was not listening to anything I said and he made it very clear that he thought I had bad etiquette. I was so hurt that he was not listening to the truth I spoke and would not give me the benefit of the doubt. I tried again to tell him that I was following proper etiquette by asking his permission first. His response again was that I had bad etiquette and was stealing his blackbelts. This experience hurt me deeply and I could no longer look to Aaron as my instructor. In retrospect, I saw that prior to this incident, he was canceling my private lessons, acting uncomfortable at my school, then when I asked for permission for women to get together and train, he accused me of being a blackbelt thief.

When I talked to Randy later he repeated Aaron's views. He could not betray his instructor, so I let him off the hook and left. I was really hurt. I had lost all respect for Aaron and could never accept him as my instructor again. I decided to write to Headquarters asking for a new instructor, but had to ask Aaron for permission first. I called and asked him, and he suggested we talk about it. I refused. It was too late - the damage had been done. The teacher/student relationship was shattered. Aaron gave me permission to get another instructor and I sent a letter stating that Aaron was a great instructor but that we had personal differences. Grandmaster's wife called and suggested I train with Kay. I politely told her that Kay was the same rank. I could not have someone as my instructor whose only talent was forms. I have to respect someone before they can teach me. Grandmaster's eldest son SJ agreed to take me as his student and I started to train with him immediately.

Training in San Francisco

When I started training at the San Francisco school, I immediately saw a difference in the quality of training. SJ had no problem teaching women and had many high ranking and quality women blackbelts. He is an amazing teacher and makes you work on your weakest areas - in my case, forms. I am a bull in a china shop. Brute strength is easy, but to be graceful in forms is a tall order. I must tax his patience every time I train, but gradually I began to do better forms. I was amazed at the difference in myself with my training under SJ. There was such a difference in training. Aaron trained with SJ but had never taught me the same things. I began to realize that it was a blessing that Aaron and I had fallen out. I was able to get better training which made me a better teacher. As SJ's student, many doors opened for me. I have learned so much from SJ and can never thank him enough for teaching me.

Two of my students were testing for blackbelt and I got SJ's permission to let them go to Aaron's for testing. I did this because Aaron's school was closer and I was not willing to give up my friends in this area just because he and I had a falling out. I continued attending blackbelt testing at Aaron's and I went with my head held high, showed him respect and never mentioned what had transpired between us. I realized later that it was only because of his wife that Aaron even talked to me. She encouraged him to have an open mind and work this through. When I started testing for 4th degree in 2005, I started having my students test in San Francisco and stopped participating in Aaron's testings.

In the meantime, Tory had joined the Air Force. She was stationed in Texas and started training with one of the Masters in

115

Houston. When Leo and I visited her, I saw her train and realized how beautiful and graceful she was in martial arts. I could not believe I gave birth to such a talented child. Tory was getting great training and was able to transfer to San Francisco and start training with SJ. It is a real treat to see her grow in her martial arts skills. I was honored to escort her when she was promoted to 1st degree blackbelt.

Chapter 9. Spiritual healing

During the period from 1st degree to 4th degree blackbelt testing, I had many ups and downs in my soul. In May 2003, I was able to quit the last thing that represented my mother by retiring from hospital billing to teach full time. It was wonderful! Since Leo had started living with me he was able to fill the painful hole in my soul. His love and willingness to stand by me were great healing forces.

We had our ups and downs but we always worked things out. I did not like some things about him, but I had to realize that he was responsible for his actions and I was only responsible for mine. When I let it go our relationship improved. What made me stick with Leo was that he had the ability to see his faults and could actually make changes for the better. Not many people can do this but he did. The other reason was that I needed to have a man who was as strong if not stronger than me. I had to have a man I could respect and I needed to feel safe when I was in his arms.

Leo is a strong intelligent man from the streets. He is my thug and I love him. As the years went by we both got better together. I always feel a spiritual connection with him. There were times when I would buy him a small gift and he would be doing the same thing for me that day. We would come home to give our gifts and realize our intentions were connected. I can still think about calling him and pick up the phone to find that he is calling me. We have our bumps but we always work it through and continue to love each other. Like good wine we get better with age.

Because of my experiences, I could not put myself back into any Christian organization. I felt returning to a church would have recreated the same dynamics of my childhood. I would have nothing to do with that. I know there are good Christian Churches out there and good people who attend them, but I still see Churches as controlling and brainwashing even though I know that is not true of all. I just feel better walking my own path and listening to the voice in my soul. Because I did this I felt I was able to re-learn who our higher power is and that He/She always walks with me.

117

I always felt that I had one foot on the spiritual side, but I had ignored this side for many years. After all the recovery work and re-parenting and re-educating myself, I was able to create positive relationships and make decisions that kept me out of toxic relationships. Only then was the damage to my spiritual side more apparent. I was still very angry at my higher power, but slowly came to realize that the Mormon Jesus and Mormon teachings had no validity in my life. The brainwashing from these toxic beliefs and my feelings of rage at a God that never saved that little girl were misplaced because that God never existed. I had to take my comprehension of what a higher power was and throw it away.

I spent several years turning my back on "God" and telling him "screw you" because of what I had to survive but also for what so many children went through and are still victimized by. I felt the injustice of what these children are forced to live. They are being victimized in God's name to desecrate what is most precious to God. What right do these people have to so horrifically abuse children? What right do they have to take an innocent child and torture her until she is forced to split her subconscious mind, to train these subconscious alters, to make them perform satanic rituals, to force them to perform sex acts and to horrify them into not talking? This anger at the lack of justice burned in me. Who protected these children? Who advocated for their rights? These were hard issues for me to work through. My experience with the Mormon Church was of this Church rejecting my truth. I was either told "that did not happen in our true church" or "that was just a one-time occurrence." This was the level of stupidity of those in leadership positions and of members. When I spoke to the leaders, I asked them how is it that when I was in group therapy, 4 ladies who were raised in 4 different states, never knew each other until now, and had only met in therapy, had two things in common: We were raised in the Mormon Church and we had the exact same ritual abuses. There was no response from these leaders.

Most people wanted irrefutable "hard proof," which will never happen. The validation that I could not refute was that the four of us had gone through the same torture training and ritual abuse. People like my abusers are far too sophisticated to leave any evidence for legal prosecution. I always say I was screwed by the best. Mormon leaders can lick your face while pissing on your feet and make you ask for more. Those are the dynamics of the intelligent abusers in the Mormon Church who raised me. This is their way of training you to enforce the "no talk - no tell" rule.

This systematic abuse experienced by people within the Mormon Church was an undeniable validation of how widespread it was and how it passed from generation to generation; just like what had happened with my mother and her Mormon roots. They continue their systematic abuse and no one is the wiser. I had to face the fact that the Mormon Church would never take any responsibility for these abuses that took place behind its own doors. While there are many good, non-abusive and unknowing people within the church, the church hierarchy will always enforce the 'no talk, no tell rule' by instructing victims to just pray and read their scriptures. This won't solve the underlying issues. That's why I say they lick your face and piss on your feet at the same time.

Spiritual understanding

I think that when you have been brainwashed by a very specific belief and rigid rules in any religious teaching you need to separate yourself from all religion for awhile. Even after Leo came into my life I still felt an emptiness in my soul and this rage at a higher power that had betrayed me. I still did not feel a real reason to live. I had external reasons - my children, Leo, friends I really cared about - but I could not feel it inside. I had to put my anger somewhere so I put it on the Mormon Jesus. I felt in my soul that there must be a different understanding of spirituality and I began to realize that every person has their own path back to God. That path was not confined to a particular building or one person's interpretation of God. That path was individual. My path was mine alone.

My path could take me anywhere I wanted to go, show me what

I wanted to see, and teach me what I wanted to learn. I had to take my own path and discover what worked for me. Since the time I was young I had always felt the presence of Native Americans around me. I do not understand why, but they are there. I had started to attend moon circles and felt a connection for a time with the beautiful ladies of native and pagan beliefs. This path took me through many years of learning and many mistakes. I felt comfortable speaking about a higher power as 'the Universe' or 'Grandfather.' I learned about Medicine Wheels, the four directions, spirit keepers, and guardians. I learned that Christianity had taken many beautiful pagan beliefs, including the "woman beautiful," and corrupted them turning wise women and healers into witches, heathens, and women of filth. These women were persecuted by ignorant male Christian leaders through the centuries. Early Christian leaders took sacred natural events, like the equinox, and turned them into something dangerous or even evil. My eyes were opened to a greater understanding of spiritual matters. I could feel the truth of what I was learning.

The herb farm I often visited offered a class on making a medicine wheel and I learned how to set the stones to create my own medicine wheel. We did smudging and had a moment of meditation. As I meditated I could see myself at home with my own medicine wheel. This felt very real and I knew I needed my own medicine wheel and needed to get my own stones. I thought about where I would get my stones and it was as if someone was shouting inside to me that I had to get them from the river in the town in which my father was raised. I could not ignore this spiritual prompting until I got the stones from the river where my Uncle had his cabin. I wondered why it had to be those stones and all I could hear from inside was "they are a witness of my life." I do not fully understand this but accepted it. I went back to the river with Sasha and chose the stones for my medicine wheel. Sasha found a flat stone with two white lines running north to south and east to west, perfectly centered on the four directions. This has always been my center stone.

I created my medicine wheel. The ladies from moon circle came and we blessed the wheel and put prayer ties on it and prayers in the ground. This medicine wheel grounded me spiritually and for the first time I started to feel better. I would go and pray in my wheel. I remember putting a prayer tie for Leo and not long after he made changes in his life for the better. I have kept my stones everywhere I moved, but have not always been able to create the right space in each new house for my stones. My wheel is like my cornerstone spiritually, but until I can create the right space I keep them close by in my closet. Leo tries periodically to move them to the garage but I always know when they are gone and put them back. He thinks I'm crazy keeping a "bunch of rocks" in the closet, but he loves me anyway. I think that when I buy property I will be able to create my wheel and find my connection again. I miss it now but I know in time I will have it again.

Bob

As I learned spiritually, I sometimes prayed to Grandfather and Grandmother to help me to find the spark in my soul and to want to live here. Sometimes I would pray in anger at the injustice of my life and the hardships I went through. On my path from moon circle, herb lore, and Pow Wows, I met an older native man named Bob. We became friends and he adopted me as his sister. He taught me about native traditions, beliefs and hardships. I took what he taught me seriously and honored what I was taught. Tory and I went to Pow Wows with him, danced in circle and made many friends. Tory made a jingle dress and learned to jingle dance beautifully. Bob said he was a holy man from his tribe in Oklahoma. He told me his family lineage and did a naming ceremony for me. He became like family. He also had his toxic behaviors, but at first I was able to keep good boundaries. We talked about my experiences and I looked to him for some kind of wisdom, but never really found what I was looking for spiritually.

I saw that he had problems and I tried to overlook them. I saw him recreate the same dramas over and over again with people who were close to him. I tried giving him tools and encouragement to make better decisions. I think that in my own integrity I tried to be true to a friend beyond the call of duty. I had this ingrained need to be honest but I was also blinded. He lost his home and I asked Leo if he could stay with us. Leo only agreed because I wanted to help Bob. Tory and I moved his belongings to storage and moved him into our home. It was the worst thing I ever did. I watched him start the same cycle with us that he had with previous friends and housemates. I introduced him to my friends in the area and he became close with a lady who lived in the country doing presentations for schoolchildren on life in the 1800's. They would come and make candles and butter, and camp in a teepee or tent. Bob moved there and started to help with the schoolchildren. He convinced a friend of mine to buy a Tee Pee for him and promised to pay it back. He lived in the Tee Pee and helped take care of her place, but it was not long before he started again, saying she did not feed him, didn't pay him ... It was all lies.

I confronted him, but he would not take responsibility for what he was doing. He stopped paying back my friend for the Tee Pee. He made a prayer fan for Tory then started talking badly about her to all my friends. Tory was going through a hard time, having just come back from a difficult job on a cruise line that did not work out. I was trying to get her to think clearly before making decisions, but she did not need her Uncle talking badly about her to everybody. It really hurt her. When I confronted him I realized he was lying again and finally saw clearly what he was - he shits where he sleeps. He ruined his relationships with everybody.

It had been four years and I could no longer take Bob's toxic behavior in my life. I stuck with him because of my great need to find spiritual healing and understanding, but in this case it created more garbage than healing. I felt that I had done so much for him and he could only shit all over my family.

What finally tore us apart was Tory's prayer fan. I discovered he was trying to it. When I reminded him that it was Tory's and he had promised it to her, he lied and began making excuses. I really blew up at him and told him that he may shit on me but he was not going to hurt my daughter ever again and he had better give that fan back. I told him he was nothing but a sell out. He used his heritage to get people to like him and handed out his traditions to get what he wanted. If he did not leave the fan where I could collect it the next day I would have the police arrest him for stealing. There would be no turning back once I made that call. I would press charges. The fan was waiting for me the next day and I took it to Tory. That fan belonged with her.

Brooke

Looking back I am embarrassed that I took the time for Bob. My own needy soul blinded me. I had the image that all native people are spiritual healers and I was trying to find that in Bob. It was not there in him and I learned from this. Like everyone, they have their issues, trials, strengths and weaknesses. They are human. It also clarified for me that I did not need to be a native person or hold native beliefs to heal. Only I could heal myself.

I still felt spiritually empty. However, through my relationship with Bob I met a gay couple, Steve and Gary. Gary was a very spiritual man and did some tarot card readings for me that helped me to put myself in the right direction. They introduced me to Brooke, a Native American and Scottish woman. Gary told her I was in great pain spiritually and needed her help. I saw that she was somewhat apprehensive, but she finally agreed. I started to see her once a month. At first I did not really trust her and wondered how she could help me. I still had a lot of anger and she could see it. She talked about native and Celtic traditions and taught me to create a sacred space and pray to the creator.

I did not want to be misled by anybody again and just wanted to take the tools and heal myself. It was hard to take the first steps in trusting anybody to heal my soul. I had to heal the spiritual damage that my parents had done to me. It took a year with Brooke to make any real breakthrough. I had to walk through all the things she was teaching me and I had to believe that she was there for me. I had to feel it within and KNOW that it was right for me.

She taught me how the pentagram was also used for good. I saw the parallel with what I had lived through and how what was abusive could also be used for good. One was for bad intentions, the other for good. I was beginning to see the balance in spiritual matters. I had a clearer picture of how Christianity tore many good beliefs apart and made them into something evil for their own ends. I was starting to feel the spark inside me come alive. She began to see a difference in me. She asked what had happened and I told her that I knew I was walking the correct path. Once I could feel that I was going in the right direction I was able to begin healing the damage in my soul.

I began to work with the tools she gave me. My path of healing began in earnest and I saw a difference in myself. As the months went by I would think about things and listen to my soul and begin to hear that small voice speak to me. As I thought a lot of things through, it became clear to me that life was life. I began to view all religious beliefs, even Christianity, as philosophies rather than "end all" truths.

I cannot stress enough how important it was for me to free myself from the toxic chains of religious brainwashing and the loss of my own autonomy. The internal "hecklers" impressions of a higher power "ready to strike you down" when you make any mistake are false. I have reconciled myself to the fact that if that higher power is one of vengeance then s/he will have his/her hands full with me. I will never accept anything less than compassionate, unconditional love. When you free yourself from this thinking you are able to understand that your Higher Power is not one of vengeance but of love. A higher power can only be understanding and unconditionally loving with no judgments when we make mistakes, when we get angry, when we fall, or when we walk in a bad way. This higher power is not limited to one teaching, one religious belief, or one way of life.

To explain my perceptions of a higher power, I'll talk about Malcolm. Three years ago, Leo's son Malcolm came to stay with us, bringing his girlfriend and her four children. The youngest was Malcolm's son and she had another on the way. Malcolm was not taught how to take care of himself. His mother took drugs and only used people to make her life work. She used her father until he died and both her sons had to move out and take care of themselves. Both boys were in gangs and in and out of jail. When Malcolm came, we made it very clear that he and his girlfriend had to find their own place to live and he had six months to get himself established. This did not happen. Neither knew how to take responsibility for themselves and used people to get what they wanted. His girlfriend finally moved to her father's house on the east coast and Malcolm stayed behind.

I helped Malcolm to write a resume, go to temporary agencies, and learn skills to take care of himself. He soon started back to drugs and street life, but I told him that if he wanted to stay in our home he had to either be in school or working. He needed to make a decision about which way his path would go, and would not recreate what he had at his grandfather's. He was not going to use Leo and me for a home to stay in while being drunk or drugging all day. This had been clear from the beginning, but he could not do it. He continued re-creating what he was familiar with. I told him he was better than that. I would ask him, "What are you doing to make your life happen?" When it came time to make that decision, he chose to be angry at his dad and blame everything on him. Leo had nothing to do with it.

I took him, taught him, helped him, and stood by him. He left angry at his dad but could not be angry at me. Deep inside he knew I was trying to help him but he was not ready for it. I still love him and want what is best for him. The love is there and the door is open. I may not agree with his choices, but I love him all the same. He could not see what I did for him and needs to walk his own path until he can see it. The love is there and always will be. This is similar to my understanding of a higher power, that loves you and stands by you no matter what our choices are in life, but expects you to take responsibility for your actions. When you think about this, decide for yourself what is best for YOU.

125

Chapter 10. Giving back what was never mine

A couple of years went by as I grew, learned and healed spiritually. I was able to understand and begin healing my soul from what my parents had done to me. I found a stick that spoke to me and kept it in the house. I would not let Leo get rid of it and if I saw it slowly moving towards the trash can I would rescue it and put it back in my closet He thought I was crazy, but he loved me and let me have my stick. After four years I finally made that my prayer stick. I took my prayer fan, medicine bag and prayer stick to Brooke and had them blessed. Through working with Brooke, I was building a foundation of spiritual growth and healing within myself.

In October 2005, I was in the doctor's office trying to make an appointment for Leo to get his drivers license renewed. I was under some stress with finances, and got really angry when the receptionist would not give Leo an appointment. I discovered that the medical group had sent me to collections and would no longer take anyone related to me for any medical care. I'd had an auto accident and instead of waiting for the insurance settlement as promised, they had blacklisted me. I hate medical groups that lie and treat you poorly. Leo needed a check-up to get his license. Without his license he could lose his job. I blew up at the receptionist and started yelling so loudly that she had to call the police. I could not believe that I lost my temper like that. I took a time out and started breathing exercises. When the police came I apologized, feeling very embarrassed. I did not usually act like this. I had better skills and knew how to make decisions when I was stressed. I went home and thought about what was going on inside.

I felt there was something wrong inside, and I decided to go back into counseling to deal with it. I had not been in therapy for almost eight years and here I was back again. I was too far away to go back to Sarah, so I found someone closer. Her name was Yvette and I liked her right away. I could tell she was a grounded and earthy person with a beautiful soul. I vetted her with several questions and decided she would be the right person for me to work with. I went to her

126

once a week to talk about my anger. I realized I had this "monkey" on my back and it had my father's name all over it. I could see that I needed to get rid of it, like a bag of garbage that was not mine. I was facing a part of my spiritual healing that still needed to take place.

After a couple of months I decided that this anger represented everything my parents did to me. I realized that their actions and life choices were not mine and were not me. Who I was did not represent what my parents did in their lives, especially to me. My father had died in 1986. As far as I knew my mother was still alive. I had not had any contact with any family members for over fifteen years. I did not care if my mother was dead or alive. I had no feelings about her one way or the other. If she was dead, I thought at least other children would not be abused by her any more. I began to see that I needed to take this emotional garbage that I had worked through and give it back where it came from. I needed a ceremony to give this back to my dad at his grave.

Though I have spent many years in therapy, I never really connected to art therapy, writing and burning, or banging a pillow to vent anger. I would try, but I could never really understand such methods. I was somewhat patronizing to anyone who talked about or encouraged me to try them. When I restarted therapy, Yvette encouraged me to try art therapy. My first response was "Okay, here we go again." Then I felt a willingness inside, so amused myself with "Sure, lets do this." I chose painting and found myself connecting with this approach for the first time. I spent time in therapy painting and drawing pictures representing my life growing up. I then painted about my life today. I saw such a difference in my paintings of childhood and my current life, that it really sunk in how much I have achieved and changed in my life.

I continued art therapy for several months, getting ready to give back all the abuse. I spoke to Brooke about what I was doing and she was very positive, saying that she would help me with a ceremony. I set a date for 2006, and spent time thinking about what I was feeling on a spiritual level. I realized that I had grown so much and been able to define my life free from anything that I grew up with. I had been able to nurture who I am and allow that part of me to grow. Because of this growth it was inevitable that what had happened during my childhood would separate from me and become a piece of garbage that needed to be put back where it belonged. This garbage was the actions and abuses of my parents, that clearly has nothing to do with who I am or ever was. It was time to give what they did back and close that door.

Closing the door

The time had come to give back what my parents did to me. I was feeling better inside and looking forward to dumping this. I knew that my life was "mine" and no longer belonged to the abuses of my parents. In preparation I took my prayer staff, prayer fan and medicine bag to Brooke and we blessed them as my spiritual tools. I wrote a letter to my father for the ceremony. It took me two weeks, but I finally had ready what I wanted to say.

On the day we'd chosen, Brooke, Yvette, Tory and I went to the town where my father was raised. At the graveyard I showed Tory her relatives. When I came to my paternal grandmother's grave I started to cry. I could feel her next to me, supporting me in what I was about to do. I had never cried before when visiting her grave. My father had not allowed me to go to her funeral, though I never understood why. I realized how much I really missed her and remembered how we would play 'go fish' or marbles on a board my father made. My grandmother did not like my older sister and never gave her presents, but always got them for her grandsons. My father did not care that my sister was rejected, as his sons were the important ones. When I came along, my mother told my dad that grandmother could not treat me the way she did my sister. My father made her be nice to me. When we played card games I could always guess her cards. It was a spiritual gift and I was only 4 or 5 years old. She would get angry sometimes, tip over the card table, accuse me of cheating, and kick me out of the house. I was not cheating and I did not realize what I was doing. She did not understand spiritual gifts and thought it as cheating. I was grateful for any chance to be free from my parents and usually wandered around town for an hour or two before going back to grandma's. She would let me in and we would start playing cards or marbles or she would take me out to lunch. I loved eating sugar cubes at her house and still remember her black bathtub and toilet. I loved my grandma and for the first time I cried for her and missed her. She was not much but she was my good grandma and I loved her.

After I showed Tory her family we went back to Yvette and Brooke. I began looking for my father's grave. I thought it was near the road but it was not. I found my uncle's grave and saw that my aunt was still alive. I remembered my other uncle's grave and saw that his wife too was still alive. Both ladies were about ten years older than my mother so would be close to their 90's. I finally found my father's grave, which was not where I remembered it. It disturbed me and I thought maybe they moved it, as I remembered the grave-side service being next to the road. It shook me. Maybe I do not remember correctly or maybe I was made to remember incorrectly, another validation of the control they had over me.

Brooke started to smudge the area and create a sacred space. She gave us each a paper explaining the ceremony and what we needed to do and say. That is the one thing I really respect about native traditions. They are not based on rigid rules but on your intentions. You can create your ceremony from your heart and it will be good. Your relationship with the creator is between you and the creator, no one else. All of us stood around my father's grave. As we performed the ceremony Tory started to feel ill. She said she could feel my father writhing in pain, having to face the truth of his own actions. The time came for me to read my letter and give it all back. This is what I wrote:

What you took and what is not mine
You took my innocence, my life, my love, my being, my childhood, my teens, my self worth and my 20's. You took my right to choose my life. You shattered my spiritual gifts for your selfish needs and

129

gains to make you look powerful to others. You taught me that you were all powerful and I was nothing. I was only a piece of crap to serve you. You humiliated me by passing me around to other members in a sex ring, having dogs rape me when I was little. Tying me to the kitchen table and torturing me. You hung me in the garage when I said no to "making daddy happy." You forced me to split my mind so you could continue with even more heinous atrocities to ensure that I could not tell when I was out of the house and you could never be caught. I would wish my real parents would come and get me because I knew inside that you could not be my real parents. Real parents do not hurt their children. You took from me my ability to make friends, to have girlfriends, to go out and have fun. All I ever had were other kids teasing me, hitting me, hating me for reasons I never understood nor why. Never realizing you were the reason why this happened. But what can you say it was what you wanted so you could continue your heinous and gross life style you needed and willfully wanted. When I was bad in your mind you punished me by locking me in a chest of snakes, hanging me by my wrists what ever you could think of you did it. But I never gave in. I remember being little and you and others hitting and humiliating me. I remember thinking that one day I will be big like them and I WILL MAKE THEM STOP.

You tried to carry on your heinous practices to my children. You hurt my children and especially Mark. But I stopped you. I started to get a hold of my life and I stopped you. That really scared you because you knew what a fighter I was. You knew that if I began to remember I would not be stopped in taking my life back. You knew I would talk. You tried very hard to stop me by trying to kill me. Turning the Mormon Church against me (which was the best thing you ever did). But it did not work because Grandfather, Grandmother, the Adepts, Gods & Goddess, Spirit Keepers and all who saw me and helped me to survive stood by me and kept me and my children safe. So here I am, this is your shit, your garbage, your life that you pursued with every willful choice you made regardless of the damage and consequences it may take on any life. It was yours to choose and you chose it. So here it is.

I no longer want or need this in my life. I have taken my life and have put in me what is ME, what is beautiful that life offers. I will-fully choose life that is beautiful and spiritual with no fears. Let me tell you what I have achieved.

I can make friends in any circle of life. I have defeated the hecklers ingrained in my subconscious you put in my mind that never give me a chance to believe in myself and that I can achieve! I defeated my personal fears, my lack of hope, lack of self worth lack of trust, lack of love, and lack of my being. I truly believe in and can say the words out loud; "I respect myself too much to allow you to do this to me." I internalized in me that it does not matter that I used disas-sociated survival skills; it only means that I was intelligent and I had the skills to survive you. I also have the skills and intelligence to take my life back.

I have done all of these things. I have friends in many circles; I do not need counseling all the time. But I have the wisdom to know when I do. I am a Gardener; I love to be in the country, to feel the earth. I love all animals and plants. I love my horses sooooo much. They are the anchor in my life that takes all of my stress away and makes me happy. I love communicating with horses. I know I am a warrior spirit; it is easy for me to rise up and fight for what is right. I have no fear of this. I fought for my life everyday growing up with you in it. I have learned to take the warrior side in me and find a place through martial arts to let it shine. I accept who I am, the warrior woman and the beautiful woman. I love herbs and heal-ing herbs that our mother earth gives us to live. I am a spiritual being with spiritual gifts that you abused but now are mine. My spiritual gifts are no longer in pain, nor am I scared to see that side of me. My spiritual gifts have healed, growing, learning and no longer afraid. I walk this earth of my free will. I have a real man that loves me beyond all measure. He has stood by my side and never left. He has loved my children and is their dad. He raised them and showed them what a man and loving father should be. I have many people in my life that accept me and love me. I am the

*warrior who fought you, I am the warrior who never gave up and I
am the warrior you feared everyday I took remembering what you
did. I am the warrior and the beautiful woman who no longer has
nor carries your garbage. There is no place in my life for you.*

Shelby Rising Eagle

When I finished reading the letter, Brooke had me dig a hole and
put my letter in his grave. Then Brooke asked the creator to give this
back to my father. Just as she said this I could hear the beating of
wings. I saw two ravens fly very low between all of us in circle. They
seemed to take away what my parents had done to me, flew between
all of us in circle and then flew away. I could feel the doors close behind me on represented their abuse and see spiritual light in front of
me. It was like opening a door that showed a bright essence of what
my life held for me.

Retirement and my own horses

I retired from medical billing in 2003, hoping never to return
again. I had a successful school through the parks department and
was able to devote my time to teaching and doing what I loved. I
did not make much money, but I loved to teach and Leo finally had
a steady job. I could afford to quit my day job. When I quit everybody saw a dramatic change in me and told me how much happier I
looked.

I have loved horses since I was a little girl and they were very important to me. Not long after I retired I asked Mary if she needed
help turning back cows. The answer was a resounding yes, so every
Tuesday and Thursday morning we loaded up the horses and went to
help Doug train. For three years Mary and I had a blast turning back
cows and going to lunch. I had many great times with Mary, and I
learned so much about cutting.

When I started riding again Leo saw a huge change in me. He
saw a different side to me and how much happier I was when I could
ride. I decided to have horses in my life again. I finally was in a

position to have what I loved, the same beautiful horses from God's stable. In 2004 while turning back cows I leaned over to Mary and asked her which one of her horses would be best for me. She recommended Monty, Jessa's baby out of her quarter horse stud Tuff. Monty was a chestnut yearling, a great horse with an easygoing manner, and intelligence. I trusted Mary's recommendations with horses. The woman is a wealth of knowledge and I only wanted to learn more every time she spoke. I wrote her a check for Monty and named him Lil Mac. Mary was surprised to see me buy him.

I worked with Lil Mac and with two other yearlings Flash and Sparkle. Flash was wild eyed and spirited, the opposite to Lil Mac. He had the same great looks as his dad and I fell in love with him. Leo thought I'd lost my mind but supported me and promised to learn to ride so we could do it together. I ended up buying Flash along with Lil Mac. I did all the groundwork with them and learned many things from Mary. On my last horse in Arizona, I was doing dressage up to 4th level. I wanted to do cutting and reining with both of my boys when they were older. So this was a complete change for me. It has been a tough transition but I am getting there.

Mary decided to sell her ranch and move to a small town in Northern California. She was tired of so many city people moving to the country and all the city garbage that came with it. Our small towns are being lost to over-development. I was sad that she was moving, but knew it was the best thing for her and her husband. I cried for a few months, knowing I was losing a good friend. She had done so much for me and Tory. The loss of her daily friendship was hard to accept. However, she is so much happier in her small town. Leo and I have been to visit them and really loved it there. It was very beautiful there and nice to get away. I have realized that Mary was a great healing force in my life. She showed me that you can be a strong woman and beautiful at the same time. I cannot thank her enough for what she has done for me and for being my friend.

133

Making peace with old colleagues

I loved teaching and will always teach martial arts. As an instructor I learned that not only was I a teacher but also a person of counsel or a mentor to many students. I willingly accepted this and had the boundaries in place to not cross over between personal and professional. I have balanced how to walk with them and not own their lives. One of the things I realized was that I could hear my student's souls. I could hear their pain or happiness. I would not have to say anything and in time they would open up to me, telling me what I already saw. If I've had a bad day I can teach and it all goes away when I work with my students. I have watched several students overcome challenges in their lives and have been honored to celebrate life's ceremonies and events with them.

I still train in San Francisco and because of SJ I am a better instructor and martial artist. Every three years my style has a world competition in Korea. In 2005, I had saved enough money to watch the competition and sight-see for ten days. Aaron was there as he was getting promoted to 5th degree and would now be a master. Prior to this trip, Aaron called to tell me that one of our mutual friends, Tom, had passed away after battling cancer for several years. They had moved to Texas so she would be with his extended family after he died. Aaron started to ask about my school and how I was doing and so forth. Then he stopped and told me that he was proud of me and apologized for what had happened between us. I couldn't believe he apologized to me after three years, but inside I felt much better about the whole thing. When Aaron was promoted to Master in Korea I took pictures and remember thinking about all the years gone by and how we had watched our children grow up, have relationships, and the birth of grandkids. I remembered when he was a 1st degree blackbelt and here fourteen years later I watched as he was promoted to Master. I was proud of him and glad that he had apologized and made things right between us. We are better friends than just teacher/student and that is okay.

Kay and her daughter came to Korea as well. We still were not speaking and she had ostracized herself from many in the martial arts community. After settling into the hotel in Pusan, several of us decided to go sight-seeing. I saw Kay standing by herself in the lobby and thought, okay it has been over ten years and we cannot talk to each other. I decided it was ridiculous and went over to shake Kay's hand and ask how she was doing. She was shocked, but responded positively. We talked about our daughters and how much they have grown and achieved in their lives. That broke the ice and I made sure never to talk about the past. I hoped this thaw would continue and spent the whole trip giving kind words to her. She always responded and during the tournament we talked about people we knew and in time found a common ground from which to respect each other. I was glad I could take the first step and create a better path between us and a way to be good to each other.

I loved the Korea trip and saw what a wonderful country Korea was and how beautiful the people were. I hope one day to go back. The trip enabled me to mend friendships and make new ones. I now have friends from the schools in England and am planning for Tory and I to have a martial arts vacation in England.

Back to medical billing

By 2006 the cost of living had increased and I needed to go back to work. I also wanted to make enough to open my own martial arts facility. The economy was bad and it was a hard time to meet this goal. I did not want to do medical billing and tried to seek other means of employment. For example, I tried car sales, but could not work their extensive schedules due to my teaching responsibilities. I went back to medical billing because I could not find another job I could do that would pay as well.

I was soon working for two surgeons near where I taught. I was the only medical biller, and soon became billing supervisor with my own office. I realized that this office was in the stone age regarding office protocol and procedures. I spent a lot of time teaching them to use the internet for eligibility, to get authorizations done correctly, and bringing them up to speed on federal laws and compliances. Here I am retired from medical billing for three years and teaching them the basics. I saw that the older doctor had poor boundaries and enjoyed watching his staff squabble. The other doctor was better and smarter, so burnt out as I was I figured that as long as I would be left alone in my own office I would be okay. In time I saw that the office manager had no knowledge of running a medical office and was not interested in learning. The other two employees had no prior experience and I spent time teaching them how to do their jobs. The business had been on the brink of bankruptcy due to the incompetence of my predecessor. I cleaned up their accounts and got them current within three months time. They were getting more money and their A/R was outstanding.

At least in this office I was able to finish writing my story. I respect myself too much to allow myself to continue like this and will trust my higher power that a better job will become available as I move on with my life. I have goals and need to pay off debts so I will continue to work. I will attain my goal of being debt-free and teaching out of my own facility.

My children as adults

Since Tory left home and began serving in the Air Force she has grown up so much. She is a beautiful woman who is able to manage her life and live in a positive way. I am really proud of her. She has overcome many things, but she has grown from these experiences. She still drives me crazy and still does not listen, but that is normal in any mother-daughter relationship. I just walk with her and watch her grow and learn.

She has her associate's degree and is working towards a bachelor's in business. She decided that when she has finished serving our country she will get her degree in Equine Sciences and have a life working with horses. When she finished high school she just wanted to leave our small town. Now she wants to go back to the country and have that lifestyle. Once she has her masters degree she can work anywhere she wants. She will be able to take care of herself and live the life she wants.

She still trains and is a graceful and talented martial artist. She bought a beautiful quarter horse filly from Mary, who is a sister to Flash. I call her Lil Momma and Leo and I love her. Lil Momma's personality is just like Tory's. They are both beautiful but picky about who handles them. They have kindred spirits and belong to each other. I cannot believe I gave birth to such a wonderful daughter. She is a bright light in my life. Looking at her I see what I could have been if I had not been so horrifically abused. She is beautiful and has her life ahead of her.

In 1999 Mark turned eighteen. He decided he did not need medication anymore and that I was not a person he wanted in his life. He had overcome so much in therapy. He was able to manage his life, but still needed support and his medications. He was finally able to mainstream into regular classes and graduated from high-school. His diagnosis now is Schizophrenia. When he does not have his medication his thinking gets distorted and delusional. He told the people in his care home that I was bad and he did not want to see me any more. It really broke my heart. I had done all the right things by protecting him and making sure that he got all the help and care he needed. I did not think that when you did all the right things as a parent you could still lose your child. It was hard for me to accept that he no longer wanted me around. I cried a long time.

He had to move to an adult care home when he graduated from high-school and no one could tell me where he went. He was an adult and they had to respect his decisions. I was devastated and only had my prayers to Grandfather to keep him safe. I did not hear from him for four years. As I prayed for my son I could feel that small voice in my soul that said he was okay and to wait, but it was hard "not knowing." I had to trust my higher power. One day in 2003 I pulled up to the park after Tory and I had finished teaching a class, and I saw Mark. I pulled over and started crying. Tory wanted to know what was wrong. I said "Look" and she saw Mark. I was afraid that if I went over to him he would run away, so I asked Tory to talk to him. Mark was glad to see her and wanted to see me as well. I got out of the car crying and gave him a big hug. I asked where he lived and he said he'd just moved to a group home and came to the park for exercise.

I was thrilled that he was there and wanted me in his life. I still do not know what happened during those four years. He does not talk about it. The important thing was that I could start my relationship with my son again. I picked him up when I taught class and he would exercise in the park. We go out to eat at a Chinese Buffet every two weeks. We have a great relationship and do what we love - eat food. He needs to stay in an adult care home due to the support and medications they provide, but he comes home for holidays and birthdays and is able to have a better life.

I get sad from time to time about Mark. I really believed that I could help him overcome his disabilities but I could not. I wish he could have a normal life like Tory, but it was not meant to be. It is hard to see him on so many drugs and I wonder what toll it will take on his long-term health. I wish I could wave a magic wand and make him better but I can't. Every life has a purpose and a meaning. Because of his disabilities he saved my life and I can never thank him enough for being my son.

Conclusions

I find myself in a good place. The door has finally been closed and I now have nothing but the future in front of me to create as I see fit. I have worked through the abuse memories. I learned problem solving, verbal and communication skills and effectively use them. I now manage my life and can handle everything that comes my way. I may not like what comes my way but I will handle it. I can make mistakes and that is ok. I feel in my soul a reason to live and want to live my life. I no longer see myself as the person on the outside with the extreme abuse issues. I am a survivor of heinous atrocities and I claim my right to my life and I live it. I have healed my spirit. I walk my path connected to the creator and the creator walks with me. When I walked away from my family not knowing what lay ahead of me the Creator made a path of healing for me. Now I am loved, I have friends I love and they love me. I am no saint, I still make mistakes. I still shoot from the hip and put my spades on the table in my everyday life. The reason why? Life is hard enough when you are right with yourself so why make it worse by lying and playing mind games with the people you interact with. I still have the urge to use violence to deal with things but I choose not to because I have learned better ways.

As I have gotten older I have more wisdom. I learned more refined ways of dealing with things. I am still rough around the edges, but I have smoothed out the spikes. I would love to have a college degree and become a profiler.

I have learned that I love gardening and feeling connected to the earth. I love teaching martial arts and being successful at it. I will continue to do what I love the most. Ride my horses and do cutting and reining with the hope of finding success. In time I want to live on 20 acres in a very small town, grow my own foods, learn to be self sufficient and be left alone with just Leo and me. I want to find my connection to the earth with my medicine wheel again. The warrior woman still lives in me just as vibrant and strong as when I was little standing up to my parents and telling them to stop hurting me. From this path of healing, fighting and surviving emerged a very beautiful woman I found in me and was meant to be. The most important thing in my recovery work was stopping the cycle of abuse. My children are free from this garbage. As a mother I have passed the warrior woman to my beautiful daughter. She has taken her warrior mother's love and balanced it with her refined and graceful soul. I guess I did a good job.

Never Forget
What you did to survive you can use to heal
Love and peace in all things

Shelby Rising Eagle

Internet: http://www.howwoulduknow.com/
Twitter: https://twitter.com/howwoulduknow
Face Book: Shelby Rising Eagle

Mary's thoughts:

When Shelby asked me to proofread her second book I was happy to do so - having read the first book (How would you know - a story in poetry) and talking to Shelby, I had an idea of the kind of abuse and terror she must have lived through as a child. It's never easy to read a book such as this. It is a true accounting of a person's life - and what a person can do to once more obtain control of that life. She has been through more than any person should have to go through and still turned out to be a caring, loving person (and a bit of a goofball, I'll admit, but that's not a bad thing). I say that in only the best of ways - she's just fun to be around. Her life is a map of ups and downs, curves and straight-aways, hills and unscalable mountains, but it is also a map of integrity, truth and honor.

I can only say that I'm proud to have her for a friend.

Mary (Maralon)

References

1. Rising-Eagle, S., *How Would You Know, a story in poetry 2002.*

2. *DSM-IV-TR: Diagnostic and Statistical Manual of Mental Disorders.* 2000, Arlington: American Psychiatric Association

3. van der Kolk, B. and R. Fisler, *Dissociation & the Fragmentary Nature of Traumatic Memories: Overview & Exploratory Study.* J Trauma Stress, 1995. 8(4): p. 505-25.

4. Sinason, V., ed. *Attachment, Trauma and Multiplicity: Working with Dissociative Identity Disorder.* 2005, Routledge: London.

Made in the USA
Charleston, SC
23 February 2012